The Frequency for Health for End Times

Fiction or Non Fiction?

Dr. Kimberly A. McCowan

Table of contents

Foreword

Wow, what a book! I am honored to have the opportunity to write a forward for a book that has touched my heart and mind profoundly. "The Frequency of Survival for the End Times" by Dr. K is a work of incredible depth and significance that transcends the boundaries of fiction and non-fiction, for it speaks to the essence of our faith and humanity. From the moment I opened these pages, I was captivated by the power of Dr. K's words. This book compels you to keep reading and forsake all else because it carries a message of utmost importance. This is not just a story but a spiritual journey that will leave you on the edge of your seat. In particular, I was moved by Dr. K's chapter on Transcendental Meditation Mantras and the profound wisdom of replacing such mantras with the word of God. It is a masterful insight that holds relevance not only for those who may find themselves in challenging times but for all of us here and now. The frequencies of Acceptance, Peace, Hope, and Love, among others, explored in this book offer a blueprint for a meaningful and purposeful survival plan for those who fail to be ready for the return of CHRIST.

I have witnessed the dedication and passion with which Dr. K approached this assignment. Her unwavering commitment to this work is nothing short of miraculous. She has poured her heart and soul into this book, and the world is better for it. If you are reading this book after the events it describes have unfolded, I implore you to read it with an open heart and a sense of urgency. This is not just a tale; it is a roadmap to victory in the most challenging of times the world has ever had.

Dr. K., your work in crafting this book is nothing short of extraordinary. I am immensely proud of you, and I do not doubt that your words will touch millions of lives long after we have gone. To God be the glory for the gift you have shared with the world. Thank you, Dr. K, for your obedience to the call of God and for the transformation this work has brought you. I have seen you change right before my eyes. Your passion, care, forgiveness, and prayers for the world are a testament to your change and love for people. In closing, I want to express my hope that none of our loved ones or friends are left behind in the times this book envisions. But if they are, may they find this book as a beacon of hope and guidance to stay faithful to the King of Kings and The Lord of Lords.

With gratitude and admiration,
I Love you,
Your husband, Pastor/Prophet Lonnie G. McCown

It's such an amazing and powerful read! First and foremost, I must say that this book profoundly covers every situation and dynamic that the body of Christ is dealing with at this hour. This amazing book deals with the evangelic passion for winning souls and reaching the lost through practical living and the relational strength needed in these times and seasons. I would recommend this book to anyone looking to strengthen their inner man and their discipleship and discipline in understanding the world's frequency and systems. There is also a great release of knowledge in the science, metaphysical, and spiritual realms of the gospel, which is often not articulated as profoundly as expressed in this book, "The Frequency of Survival for the End Times."

I believe this book will reach the masses, as it is designed to reach those ready to spiritually reformat their lives and those who desire to welcome divine structure and order of the word of God and the Holy Spirit into their lives. As I read this book, it was very powerful

because I began to realize things that I had never thought of or considered a frequency that are frequencies that lead to freedom and deliverance in our lives. For example, the chapter on forgiveness is amazing, as many of us don't understand the frequency of forgiveness and the things that come in and out of our lives. So many keys in this book will unlock revelation and insight, like the frequency of meditation and declaration. I was extremely blessed when I read about the frequency of food, water, vitamins, and minerals.

Anyone working on re-establishing their health or desiring to preserve what God has given them must read this book! For it is truly designed with your destiny in mind. This book is intended for every Kingdom-minded believer willing to be open to seeing and looking outside the box. The greatest part of this read is it addresses the frequency of reaching the lost and bringing them to salvation. When we look at the word salvation in Greek, it is the word sozo where we get our word for soteriology. This book, "The Frequency of Survival for the End Times," by Dr. Kimberly McCowan, helps us understand that we must be saved, healed, delivered, rescued, and prosper on all levels of our lives.

In His Service,
Bishop, Dr. Princeton L. Allen Th.d., D.D.,
Senior Pastor
Ephraim Manasseh Worship Center

Dedication

This book is dedicated to every person who crossed my path on earth, and I did not share the message of Jesus. I write this dedication to you with deep regret and an agonizing apology for not realizing God's ultimate plan for my connection with you was to share the message of Jesus and prepare you for the rapture. I am deeply sorrowful that you have been left behind when I called you a friend and said I cared about you but didn't share Jesus with you. I am sorrowful that you have been separated from your children and grandchildren who put their faith in Jesus and have been taken up to heaven with the rapture. I am sorrowful that I was selfish in my relationship with Jesus and left you behind to suffer in a seven-year timeframe known as the "tribulation."

I apologize to all the people I attended junior high and high school with whom I didn't talk about Jesus. I apologize for disregarding your life's importance as I focused on school activities and popularity with pictures in the yearbook. I apologize to all the friends I ditched class with and hung out at the football field to smoke marijuana instead of telling you about Jesus. I apologize to all my college friends for the example I gave you as a church believer, spending weekends with you partying in the clubs instead of inviting you to church. I apologize for my selfishness, knowing my eternal destiny was secure while yours was destined for destruction. I apologize to every patient for the missed opportunities to share the gospel because I was too busy to trust God. I stopped and made time to listen and encourage you with the message of Jesus. I apologize to every person in the stores, malls, restaurants, and at the airport who felt drawn to talk to me. I was too tired or busy to give you the time of day and see the value you carried before Jesus. I apologize to all my co-workers at every job I worked with. I developed caring relationships, but I never showed how much I cared for you by talking to you about the most important relationship you can have: a relationship with Jesus. I apologize to all the doctors I worked with who poured their wisdom into me for patient care; I never shared the knowledge of God for eternal salvation with them.

I am deeply sorrowful, and for this reason, I am writing this book. I dedicate this book to all those that I missed the opportunity to share Christ with and to other people I never get the chance to meet who have been left behind to suffer seven years of "tribulation." While writing this book, I was in deep turmoil, sometimes unable to sleep for days as I struggled with the pain of my regret for not sharing Jesus with you. I pray that this book prepares you for the next seven years on earth because I failed to prepare you for the rapture in my assignment.

If you read this book and the rapture has taken place, you have been left behind. If you are reading this book and the rapture has not happened yet, you still have time. God inspired the content in this book with glimpses of the future in a "prophetic time travel" with visions of society during the tribulation. I took these visions using scriptures from the Bible to author "The Frequency of Survival for End-Times" to explain the events of the tribulation discussed in the Book of Revelations. Although many of my visions carry imagery of horrible, unimaginable persecution people will face who put their faith in Jesus, there is hope for every person who chooses to endure and put their faith in Jesus. Some people will read this book and understand the wisdom of God for direction and view the content as non-fiction, while others will read this book as pure entertainment, viewing it as fiction. While you read this book, you can choose if the book's content is fiction or non-fiction.

Introduction

My first introduction to energy and frequency was in health in 1989. My father was 50 years old and was admitted to the hospital in Intensive Care Unit (ICU). Earlier that evening, when I stopped by my parents' house, my father sat in a red-winged back chair in the corner of my parents' bedroom. He didn't look well and had been vomiting for several days, and I remember urging him to go to the hospital. It was sometime later that evening that I received a phone call from my mother telling me that my father had been admitted to the hospital in ICU, where my mother worked as a critical care nurse. The entire family rushed to the hospital and gathered in the waiting room to hear what was happening with my father. I can't remember the details of how the doctor delivered my dad's prognosis, and to this day, it's still a blur. However, I can remember being in complete disbelief when we were told my father had less than 24-48 hours to live. My dad had just turned 50 years old and always appeared healthy. However, my father acquired adult-onset asthma after his service in the military during the Vietnam War. He was treated with an endless supply of Prednisone, which resulted in Cushing's Syndrome and adult-onset diabetes. Even with asthma and prednisone-induced Cushing's Syndrome, my dad still loved ice-cream and apple pie and exercised regularly to stay in good health. The last thing I expected to hear from the doctor was my father was going to die in less than 48 hours. The doctor told our family that my father was in complete heart failure, and I was in shock and disbelief.

My father was a Pastor and ordained in the Calvary Missionary Baptist Church ministry on July 15, 1977. Since he was a gospel minister, one would expect a peaceful transition during his last hours on earth, and that was exactly how it happened. During the time leading up to his transition, my father was traveling back and forth between dimensions. It was as if he would fall asleep, exiting this dimension to travel into another dimension, and then wake up moments later to talk about what he experienced in the other dimension. My family rotated turns at my father's bedside for hours as he drifted in and out of consciousness with messages from another dimension. I don't recall everything my father talked about. Still, I clearly remember an occurrence where I sharing that his death was a tough decision, as if there was a deliberation taking place regarding his transition. It was during this encounter that my investigations of energy began.

As my father was crossing back and forth between two dimensions, I explicitly recall the message that my father spoke in clear words, *"reverse the polarity; you need to reverse the polarity."* I had no idea what my father meant and assumed his words might be related to the disease process affecting oxygen circulating to his brain. But yet, my father was never confused or restless during his transition. He was peaceful and clear in relaying messages about his experiences in his transition. Today, I believe my father was revealing an important message about energy and frequency that affects our livelihood that is often overlooked, *"you need to reverse the polarity."*

My father died on March 4, 1989, which was a few weeks before I received the results that I successfully passed the exam for a Registered Nurse from the California State Board of Nursing. As I stood alone in a condo where I was renting a room and learning that I had passed the exam for a registered nurse, tears began to stream down my face. The grief from the death of my father was so deep I felt the breath being squeezed from my lungs only to settle in my throat. As I stood there with test results in my hand and tears rolling down my cheeks, I made an unconscious vow that would define the course for my life assignment to promote health and well-being. It was during that time that I made an unconscious promise with a vengeance against sickness and disease and vowed I would care for every male patient like they were my father or brother and every female patient like it was my mother or sister. At that time, my passion for health was anchored to my soul, not to nurture sickness and disease but to encourage people to recover through a message that promotes health and well-being.

Several weeks after receiving my board results, I obtained a job with a position as an RN preceptee at St John's Regional Medical Center. I started my career in the Orthopedic/Urology Medical Surgical Unit, working under a former army nurse named Ruth Foster, who wore a pill box white nursing cap. She was instrumental in providing a solid patient care and advocacy foundation. After one year in the medical/surgical unit, I transferred to the ICU. Since my father died in the ICU and my mother worked as an ICU Registered Nurse, I felt compelled to work with critically ill patients in that area. During that time, the requirements to work in the ICU involved completing three months of didactic coursework and partnering with a preceptor with hands-on training to manage critically ill patients' care. Norma Dalton was my preceptor, and she had a deep passion for patient care that strengthened my foundation as a patient advocate. Under her guidance, I gained invaluable insights into patient care and advocacy, laying the groundwork for my future in healthcare.

During the 3-month ICU coursework, I reintroduced the concept of energy and frequency. One day, while sitting in the conference room of the didactic portion of the program, the instructor began to discuss the physiology of the heart, which functions from energy and polarity and affects how the heart pumps. When I heard the instructor continue to explain heart failure and the polarity, something hit my heart like a ton of bricks. My father's words came back to me, *"You have to reverse the polarity."* For the remaining class period, I sat in class holding back tears, making the connection to the cause of my father's death and the message to *"reverse the polarity."*

I worked in the ICU for many years, caring for and advocating for critically ill patients and their families before transferring to the emergency room. After 15 years of experience in the clinical setting, I decided to return to school for higher education. During this time, I had a dream that sparked my interest with a passion for investigating the role of energy and frequency for health and wellbeing.

In the dream, I was sitting in the ICU, and the world-renowned scientist, Albert Einstein, was watching me on the other side of a large window. He motioned me to the window and whispered something to me through the window. The window disappeared as I moved toward him, and he whispered directly in my ear. I listened intently to the soft whisper but could not make out the words. I forced myself to listen even harder, but I still couldn't make out the words of the secret message whispered to me in my ear. Reflecting on that dream and the encounters leading up to this time, I realize that I have been seeking and searching for healthy answers to preserve humankind's well-being. As I ponder Albert Einstein's famous words, "Everything is energy," I realize that they include the state of sickness, disease, and well-being, reflecting energy and frequency.

The Frequency of Survival for End Times is a book written as a tool to guide you through life during a time when the frequencies of this world go haywire. This book was written with the primary purpose of promoting well-being using the concepts of energy and frequency. In the assignment to promote health, God instructed me to author a book addressing the well-being and livelihood of people left behind after the first rapture. This book was primarily written for people as a guide for survival for people who did not surrender and accept the message of Jesus Christ and left behind to endure seven years of tribulation.

Whether you view this book as fiction or nonfiction, the content provides important information about the tribulation written in the scriptures found in the book of Revelations. Fiction or nonfiction, this book holds valuable insights and revelation from God's Word about tribulation and the concepts of energy and frequency for survival. If you are reading this book and were left behind, this book will explain how the divine energy from God flows through your body for nourishment and health. This book will be an instrumental tool for survival when accessing quality healthcare will be difficult because the anti-Christ system will require you to have the mark of the beast, pledging allegiance to trust Satan for your livelihood and survival.

The content of this book includes scriptures from the original King James Version (KJV) since the anti-Christ will attempt to ban the original KJV from mainstream society. The anti-Christ will provide an alternative version of the Bible for a One-World Religion called the Universal Bible of Inclusion, which will be the new authorized official Bible. Since the original KJV and another similar version will be removed from circulation and made obsolete, I have included scriptures from these versions that you will not find in the Universal Bible of Inclusion. I pray that this book gives guidance and insight when the Word of the Lord for instruction will be rare. The book will be important at a time when preachers and teachers who taught the gospel and the message of Jesus will be censored and removed from all social media platforms. Fiction or non-fiction, if you are reading this book after the rapture, you must understand that in all the chaos and confusion, you are holding a book that can be used as a tool that will explain the events of the rapture and tribulation and then guide you through the tribulation for livelihood and survival.

To author this book, God gave me visions of the future in prophetic time travel across time zones to glimpse what's to come and what people will face that were left behind. The context of this book was written based on the visions I received during my prophetic time travel into the future after the rapture of believers from the earth. My visions appear to align with scriptures related to the rapture and the seven-year tribulation. I am unclear if the seven-year tribulation is based on the Gregorian or Luni-solar Jewish calendar. But, based on my faith, I am most certain the rapture of the church is real; it will happen, and there will be a seven-year tribulation involving people left behind who did not acknowledge God and reject the gift of salvation. I hope and pray that this book provides insights so you can discover a divine strength within you to navigate through the world until the second rapture.

To get the most benefit from this book, you must understand that scriptures from the original versions of the Bible are the active invisible subatomic substance of God's Word that was written down as letters after being breathed from the mouth of God, who is the source of all energy.

All scripture is given by inspiration of God, and is profitable for doctrine, for reproof, for correction, for instruction in righteousness: That the man of God may be perfect, thoroughly furnished unto all good works.
2 Timothy 3:16-17 (KJV)

God's Word is the divine substance that created the frames of this world and will continue to maintain the frame of the world until God decides to make a new heaven and earth for eternity. The belief in the divine inspiration of scripture serves as a foundational tenet of faith for millions worldwide, providing spiritual guidance, nourishment for the soul, and health for the physical body to navigate the complexities of life and the pursuit of eternal truths.

Through faith we understand that the worlds were framed by the Word of God, so that things which are seen were not made of things which do appear.
Hebrews 11:3 (KJV)

The present world exists because when God spoke words, His word carried a frequency that framed the world.

God's words framed the world because divine power was frequently released with His words. For example, in

Hinduism, the Rigveda describes creation as originating from the primordial sound of "Om," symbolizing a divine power inherent in speech. That same frequency of divine power released when God spoke to frame the world is the same frequency in the Word of God you read in this book, which can be activated with a proclamation. In Tibetan culture, Tibetan Buddhist monks base their chants on the "Om" tone with a frequency of 135 Hz, which is believed to have a profound effect on relaxing the body, mind, and soul. The Word of God still carries a frequency of divine power because it is harnessed in the written Word, and just like it maintains the frames of the world, the Word of God can preserve the frame of your body for livelihood and survival when you make proclamations for a frequency of health.

20 My son, attend to my words; incline thine ear unto my sayings. 21 Let them not depart from thine eyes; keep them in the midst of thine heart. 22 For they are life unto those that find them, and health to all their flesh.
Proverbs 4:20-22 (KJV)

In my earth assignment before the rapture, I was tasked with promoting health by connecting my science knowledge and understanding God's Word, which works like medicine to heal the body because it harnesses subatomic invisible substances from the divine Creator God. Countless testimonies of people with restored strength and health because they used faith in the sacred power harnessed in God's Word. The same power that resided in God's Word before the rapture will remain in God's Word even after the rapture. This book will serve as a tool for your livelihood and survival using scriptures from the KJV Bible.

Now, here is my disclaimer as the author. This book was written to explain events surrounding the rapture and tribulation to be used as a guide for livelihood and survival. This book is not intended for medical purposes or a replacement for medical treatment but for informational and educational purposes. I have never or will ever recommend you stop any medications or treatments prescribed by your doctor, but I encourage you to use this book as a tool to support strength and for survival in the tribulation.

The concepts in this book may not be supported by evidence-based scientific studies but are based on scriptures and the foundation of the Christian faith, which can be viewed as fiction or nonfiction. And you get to your choice!

Exhortation to the 21st Century Church in America

If you are reading this book and the rapture has not occurred, I have included appeals at the end of each chapter to stimulate your faith and share the message of Jesus with everyone who crosses your path. As you read the appeals in the content of this book, please understand we are all part of the Body of Christ, and I love the church. In my service to the church, I am deeply passionate about the role of leadership. I have to see the 21st-century church operates in God's original plan to heal the sick, cleanse the lepers, raise the dead, and cast out devils to free people from a deteriorating medical system.

As you enjoy the pearls of wisdom and divine insights from this book, are confident in your salvation, and will never have to experience the horrors related to the tribulation, I challenge you to heed the exhortations for the

21st-century church in each chapter. If the rapture hasn't occurred, we still have time to share Jesus and the message of the cross so your family and friends will not be left behind and will need this book. Please, do not ever assume people do not want Jesus, especially if you have never asked them. People don't realize how much they need Jesus. So, I challenge you to share Jesus with your family and friends so they can be raptured up with you and put into eternal glory with Jesus.

You Were Left Behind

The first chapter of this book will explain the confusion and chaos caused by the worldwide disappearance of more than a billion people. In a straightforward explanation, the rapture of the church has taken place, and people who put their faith in God have been raptured to heaven, and you have been left behind. I have included a scripture reference from both the King James Version (KJV) and the Bible Message Version regarding the rapture for you to read. As previously mentioned, you will not find scriptures like this in circulation since any versions of the Bible with the message of Christ and the second coming will be taken off the internet and all social media platforms.

36 But of that day and hour knoweth no man, no, not the angels of heaven, but my Father only. 40 Then shall two be in the field; the one shall be taken, and the other left. 41 Two women shall be grinding at the mill; the one shall be taken, and the other left.
Matthew 24:36, 40, 41 (KJV)

The imagery of two people in the field or at the mill, one is taken, and the other left symbolizes the suddenness and unexpected nature of His coming. This highlights the importance of being spiritually prepared and vigilant for His coming, as it will occur without warning. The message conveyed is of readiness and anticipation, urging believers to remain steadfast in their faith and devotion, knowing they must be prepared to meet the Lord at any moment.

But the exact day and hour? No one knows that, not even heaven's angels, not even the Son. Only the Father knows.

"The Arrival of the Son of Man will take place in times like Noah's.

Before the great flood, everyone was carrying on as usual, having a good time right up to the day Noah boarded the ark. They knew nothing—until the flood hit and swept everything away. "The Son of Man's Arrival will be like that: Two men will be working in the field—one will be taken, one left behind; two women will be grinding at the mill—one will be taken, one left behind.
Matthew 24:36-41 (The Message)

In this passage of scripture, the writer is foretelling a future event of Jesus's return, referred to as the rapture. The scripture explains how people will work together; one will be taken or raptured, and the other will be left. Before the rapture, no one was privileged to know the exact timing of this event, although many people tried to make predictions based on the signs of the times. Although the Bible left us signs and clues of Jesus' coming, no- one knew the exact date but the Father in Heaven.

You must understand all the people declared missing are the result of the rapture. These people are not really missing; they have been taken to heaven to live in eternal glory with Jesus. The people who are gone have been raptured because they acknowledged the death and resurrection of Jesus as redemption from a sinful state and have been taken into an eternal destiny with the Heavenly Father. Unfortunately, you have been left behind because you failed to acknowledge Jesus as your Lord and Savior. You missed the rapture because you ignored the call to accept Jesus and live a surrendered life to share the message of the gospel.

Because you disregarded the call to Jesus, you have been left behind to navigate through a chaotic and corrupt world with trials and tribulations. You have been left behind and must learn how to navigate the tribulation. It is a difficult truth to swallow, but you must know the truth because the truth you perceive will be the truth you live by, and if you don't perceive the truth, you will believe the lie that will be perpetuated during the tribulation.

40 He hath blinded their eyes and hardened their heart;
that they should not see with their eyes, nor understand
with their heart, and be converted, and I should heal them.
John 12:40 (KJV)

Don't Believe the Lie

You were left behind, so don't believe a lie. It is critically important for you to know the truth about the rapture and what is happening in your world. You must grasp the truth as soon as possible so your eyes are not blinded and your ability to perceive the real truth is blocked.

Many people left behind will believe the lie perpetuated by stories of alien invasions, electromagnetic frequency causing dematerializing of bodies, or unusual vaccination reactions. The lies from political public officials will be well fabricated, and it will soothe anxieties with reasonings of a worldwide event that is causing chaos and confusion. Although the lies will provide some minor comfort of a global catastrophic event, their reasonings will never explain how an unborn fetus disappears out of the womb of a mother, only to leave an empty sac of amniotic fluid and a fully intact placenta. Their fabricated lies will never explain how people can disappear into thin air while leaving an empty shell of clothing in the place at the time of the rapture. They will try to explain this phenomenon using holographic technology, but nothing will make sense, and I caution you, do not believe the lie. If you believe the lie, your mind will be blinded, so you will never see the truth, and your eternal destiny will be at stake. You must know and perceive the truth.

And for this cause God shall send them strong delusion,
that they should believe a lie.
2 Thessalonians 2:11 (KJV)

The truth is the rapture has taken place, and all the babies and children that are declared missing have been raptured to heaven to be with God. The rapture has happened, and the earth has been silenced from a baby's coo and cry. You will no longer hear children making ruckus as they laugh and play in the park or school playground. This idea of children being taken in the rapture aligns with certain interpretations of eschatological events, symbolizing the innocence and purity of children.

All those who put their faith in God and attempted to live a surrendered life while on earth have been removed from the planet and raptured up to live with Jesus. Your family and friends you watched serve God are not missing. You can stop crying because they were not pulverized by an alien invasion or vaporized by chemical warfare or some advanced quantum electromagnetic technology. Your family and friends were raptured because they put their faith in Jesus. Over the next few months, you are going to hear countless stories of the sudden disappearance of people like surgeons who disappeared while operating, children who vanished from a school bus only leaving the bus driver, and airline pilots who disappeared while flying with a cargo of passengers. You will be tempted to believe the lie even after witnessing the news anchorman suddenly disappear right before your eyes. But the truth will be hidden from you. The truth will be concealed with lies.

The Emergency Medical System will be overloaded with 911 calls as people call in distress and sheer panic to make a missing person's report and request help. There will be countless personnel missing from their jobs, and the missing number of healthcare workers will cause a shortage, resulting in a healthcare crisis that will require the immediate implementation of advanced robotic technology to fill the gap caused by raptured healthcare workers. This robotic technology will promise to bring order and efficiency when healthcare is experiencing widespread pandemonium.

You need to know the truth, and the truth is Jesus is real, and the rapture has taken place, which explains the disappearance of masses of people. Your family and friends were raptured to be with Jesus, and they have been preparing for this great day for many years. Those of us that have been raptured began to understand the imminent return of Jesus when the recitation of school-sponsored prayer was prohibited in public schools. The signs and clues of the rapture became more evident with the implementation of the cashless system during the COVID-19 pandemic, laying the economic infrastructure for the tribulation that a one-world government will enforce for commerce, healthcare, travel, and national religion. We have been seeing the signs of rapture for some time, and now what has been declared for thousands of years has finally happened, and the prophecy of Jesus' return has been fulfilled.

The Holy Spirit has been Removed from the Earth

Your friends and family who placed their faith in God have been taken to heaven.

Although you may be experiencing deep loss and grief from a glorious event for believers, the most devastating part of the rapture for those left behind is that the Holy Spirit has been removed from the earth. Because you rejected a relationship with Jesus, you never had the opportunity to know the person of the Holy Spirit. Surprisingly enough, many believers didn't know the Holy Spirit either, and even though they made it into heaven, they would spend the rest of their eternity in the outer courts of heaven.

If you have never heard about the Holy Spirit, it was the existence of God that was given as a gift to believers who put their faith in Jesus. The Holy Spirit moved about the earth to guide believers in living right through convictions of the heart. The Holy Spirit's primary role was to support believers as a teacher, guide, comforter, and counselor to those who professed their faith and the finished work of Jesus Christ.

And I will pray the Father, and he shall give you another Comforter, that he may abide with you forever;
John 14:16 (KJV)

But the Comforter, which is the Holy Ghost, whom the Father will send in my name, he shall teach you all things,

The Holy Spirit also manifested Himself in power for miracles, signs, and wonders when teaching about Jesus. Throughout the ages, the Holy Spirit has demonstrated His presence through miraculous deeds, affirming the message of salvation and the authority of Jesus. His power, evident in signs and wonders, attests to the divine origin of Christ's mission, drawing hearts closer to the transformative grace in Him.

But ye shall receive power, after the Holy Ghost is come upon you: and ye shall be witnesses unto me both in Jerusalem, and in all Judaea, and in Samaria, and unto the uttermost part of earth. **Acts 1:8 (KJV)**

In addition to your family and friends being raptured, the Holy Spirit has also been removed from the earth. The Holy Spirit's absence from the earth means the comfort, guidance, and power that the Holy Spirit provided will not be readily available to you, and you will be forced to rely on your own strength and power to live and be a witness as you make your stand for Jesus. Although you will have angelic assistance, the fight will be more tenacious, and you will need to stay mentally strong and physically healthy.

Along with the Holy Spirit being removed from the earth, the restraining power of the Holy Spirit that held back evil forces will no longer be set in order, and every evil work will prevail where you now experience more of the dimensions of hell than in the history of time. You will no longer be able to trust in the goodness of mankind because the goodness and light that lived in believers will be removed from the earth, and every evil work will lead to a society of mass corruption.

And now you know what is restraining, that he may be revealed in his own time. For the mystery of lawlessness is already at work; only He now restrains will do so until He is taken out of the way.
2 Thessalonians 2:6-7 (NKJV)

And you know what is restraining him now so that he may be revealed in his time. For the mystery of lawlessness is already at work. Only he who now restrains it will do so until he is out of the way.
2 Thessalonians 2:6-7 (ESV)

Subsequently, with the Holy Spirit's restraining power removed from the earth, evil will prevail, and darkness will reign. As the restraining influence of the Holy Spirit is withdrawn, the forces of lawlessness loom ominously, poised to seize upon the void left in His absence. In this era of spiritual upheaval, survival becomes paramount, requiring a profound understanding of humanity's divine origin and potential. Your primary goal is for survival, and you must think about survival until the second coming. For survival, you must understand the significance of your creation and that you are an original creation of God. As an original creation, you were made in the likeness and image of God, with His divine power flowing through your physical body.

Unfortunately, humanity has limited the physical body's capabilities, failing to acknowledge a divine power that operates in the body that allows the physical body to function way beyond the limit we set. You must know you are an original creation of God and then learn how to access the divine power in you for a frequency of survival.

An Exhortation to the 21st Century Church in America

I write these words to the 21st Century Church with a deep passion in my heart for the church we call the Body of Christ. You are the church, and if you are not actively evangelizing and sharing the gospel with everyone around you, the church is in a sad state. We are the church and in a tragic state if social media platforms are used to broadcast profound messages throughout the week, but when the lights and camera turn off, our sensitivity to people in sharing the love of Jesus with those around us also turns off. We are the church and in a sad state when men and women of God can stand behind the church pulpit on Sunday morning to preach or sing to move people with emotion, but when they step off the church platform, they leave the message on the pulpit; never taking the message of Jesus to the world of their everyday environment. The church is in a sad state when many of our family, friends, and co-workers will be left behind to suffer a tortuous death because we failed to be patient with them, to love them, to pray for them, and to keep sharing the message of Christ in-spite of their resistance. While in our religious activity, we grew impatient and frustrated with them. And because the 21st Century Church turned its back, walked away, and failed to be the church, our family and friends will have to suffer the consequences of the tribulation.

Have you ever considered the people you tried to share Jesus with rejecting the message you shared on Sunday because of the example of Jesus you gave them Monday through Friday? Have you ever considered people's resistance to the message of Christ was not just the devil blinding their eyes, but the lifestyle as a "Christian" confused them and clouded their vision of the true picture of the church? The 21st-century church became comfortable and complacent, sitting on padded chairs and using structured services. The 21st-century church has grown cold with selfish agendas of how to capitalize on relationships in the church for personal validation and gain in business endeavors rather than appreciate the church for God's intended purpose to build up and equip saints in a kingdom mindset and then to mobilize the gospel of the good news to bring others into the knowledge of the kingdom of God.

If the rapture has not occurred yet, you still have time. We still have time as a church to get it right and get back on track with the original purpose and plan God ordained the church to be for this time. But first, we, the church, must repent and ask for forgiveness for missing the mark in our role as the 21st Century Church on earth. Secondly, let's ask God to remove selfish motives we may be carrying that cloud the mind from divine insights for the call to the great commission and to advance the Kingdom of God. Lastly, let's pray and ask God to increase our capacity of compassion and love so we as the church can be the true church, not just on Sunday mornings in the pulpit and behind the camera. Still, we have lifestyles of worshippers that reflect the love of Jesus every day of the week and affects everyone we meet.

The Divine Frequency of Health

In order to understand the ability and means for your survival, you must know you harness a divine frequency for health. When God created humanity, God formed and structured the outer frame of humans from the dirt of the ground.

And the LORD God formed man of the dust of the ground and breathed into his nostrils the breath of life; and man became a living soul.
Genesis 2:7 (KJV)

Throughout history, various cultures and religions have also recognized the special nature of humanity, often attributing its origin to divine acts. In the Judeo-Christian tradition, the scripture not only details man's formation from the earth by God's own hand but also underscores his distinctiveness through the infusion of a living soul. This gift sets humans apart from all other forms of creation. Genesis 2:7 will likely be another verse that will be removed from the Bible as advanced technology will introduce another species that will intermingle with the original human race in an attempt to procreate another class of species. You must understand and appreciate your uniqueness and genetic makeup as a human being, which is made in three parts: physical body, soul, and spirit. You are an original species of Adam made by God the Creator. The creation of man has been under attack for decades from arguments of evolutionary theorists that suggested man evolved from a process of evolution. With the various theories on the creation of humans, you must understand the uniqueness of your creation by God and being an original creation of the human race.

Even though advanced technology has discovered the genetic coding to create living beings, technology has failed to make a living soul. Because advanced technology cannot create a living soul, frequencies are harnessed from the cosmos to embody and bring life to their created beings. You must understand your uniqueness in the human class, which involves your creation by God as a tri-part being. And You are a spirit being, and the real you are the spirit part of you. You have a soul with a collective consciousness from this world that uses the mind, will, imagination, intellect, and emotions to process life events. The soul is often interchanged with a mind that must renewed from the world's collective consciousness to a kingdom of God mindset found in the Word of God. Your spirit and soul exist through a physical body. The physical body is not the real you but houses the spirit and soul to experience life on earth.

Now may the God of peace Himself sanctify you completely; and may your whole spirit, soul, and body be preserved blameless at the coming of our Lord Jesus Christ.
1 Thessalonians 5:23 (NKJV)

In God's original creation, God created humanity, which consists of a spirit, soul, and physical body. As a spirit being with a soul, you exist through a physical body that solely functions by the energy that came from the divine breath of God that was blown into the first man at creation, Adam. The human race is a unique species created with properties from the heavenly God. Any other species created outside of God's original plan was created by taking substance from God's original creation. It is not part of God's plan but has been made possible through science, technology, power, and greed.

Through DNA research, advanced technology has discovered a way to create another species of existence using material from God's original creation. Although this new species of human existence may or may not differ in human features, the sole difference of this new species will be the absence of a human soul because advanced technology cannot create a living soul that consists of the will, imagination, memory, emotion, and intellect. Through artificial intelligence, superbeings can be made with algorithms of a soul with programmed human responses that enhance with every human encounter. But since this species does not have a living soul, it will not have the ability to demonstrate heartfelt emotions of love, compassion, and hope that was poured into the hearts of mankind and will eventually dominate the earth.

And hope maketh not ashamed; because the love of God is shed abroad in our hearts by the Holy Spirit Ghost which is given unto us.
Romans 5:5 (NKJV)

This new species will be void of heartfelt emotions that have been poured into the hearts of God's original creation by the Holy Spirit. Although this species will have heightened awareness, superior intelligence, and highly skilled abilities that surpass the original human race made with algorithms of collective consciousness for logical reasoning, the species will be deprived of a human soul with heartfelt emotions.

You must understand that as a part of the original human species fearfully and wonderfully created by God, you are a unique species of a human class with original properties from the Divine Creator. As a species from the original human class, you are unique and have been made fearfully and wonderfully in the image of God with properties from the Divine Creator called energy.

When God created the original man, He used earth's substance and formed the physical body for man's spirit and soul to occupy their existence on earth. When God blew his breath into the physical structure made of earth's substance, the divine power of God flowed from God through that physical structure for life.

And the Lord God formed man of the dust of the ground and breathed into his nostrils the breath of life; and man became a living soul.
Genesis 2:7 (KJV)

You are a unique creation because God has created you with a soul, and you have the breath of life from God flowing through your body. This breath that brought life to the first man at creation is the same divine power that has been transferred down through the generations to all mankind in the original human race. You are a descendant of Adam from an original Adamic human class.

I will praise You, for I am fearfully and wonderfully made; Marvelous are Your works, And that my soul knows very well.
Psalm 139:14 (NKJV)

The Creator God has wonderfully and fearfully made you. You are so unique that the angels of the Lord were so intrigued by God's original creation they asked, "What is this man you created? He is like a god with creative power from the divine." This divine curiosity mirrors the broader scriptural theme where humanity is not only the pinnacle of God's creation but also a being endowed with attributes reflecting the Divine. The creation narrative, described in the scriptures across different faith traditions, highlights this special endowment. Such distinctions place humanity in a unique position of responsibility and privilege, tasked with the stewardship of the earth and cultivating the gifts imbued by their Creator, affirming the celestial interest in the potential and purpose of human life.

What is man that You are mindful of him, And the son of [earthborn] man that you care for him? Yet You have made him a little lower than God. And You have crowned him with glory and honor.
Psalm 8:4-5 (AMP)

You are a one-of-a-kind creation that cannot be reduplicated by technology. You are the original earthborn creation of God, made with His breath flowing through your body in the form of divine energy that brings life to the physical body and allows the physical body to function. Everything works in the physical body because God's divine energy flows through the body, which gives life. Let's explore this truth of divine energy flowing through the body. 1) Your muscles maintain strength and motion because God's divine energy sends impulses through your brain and spinal cord. 2) Your heart pumps because God's divine energy flows through the heart's chambers in electrical impulses that cause the heart to contract and pump blood through your body. 3) God's divine energy allows synapses in the brain to occur in circuits so you can process emotions, think, and allow messages to be carried through the cells for bodily functions. 4) God created almost every cell in your body with over 600,000 specialized structures called mitochondria that make energy for the body. These little structures make enough energy to power up seven 10-watt light bulbs when you are at rest.

Everything in your body works because God's divine energy flows through your body. When everything functions properly, the power in the body is measured in the frequency of megahertz (MHz). When the divine energy is flowing effectively through the physical body, the frequency of health is suggested to be measured at 62-78 MHz; when the frequency of the body drops below 58 MHz, the body becomes receptive to sickness and disease, and when the MHz drops below 42 the physical body becomes receptive to cancers. You are an energetic being filled with the light or *Phos* for life from God's divine energy.

> *You are the light of the world.*
> **Matthew 5:14a (NKJV)**

Because you were made in the image of God, the Light with no darkness in Him, you are an energetic being created with light or *Phos* from God the Creator. To maintain strength and health in the physical body, you must learn how to keep *Phos* energetically charged with a frequency so that light can illuminate the body's cells for health. You must know how to keep the body at a frequency for health of 62-78 MHz The frequency of health is not a new concept and has been in circulation for many years, only to be adopted by the New Age, rejected by the Christian faith, and dismissed as pseudoscience. However, the intent of the content in this chapter goes beyond the concepts of the New Age in raising your vibration level; it provides the understanding that you are an original creation of God with divine energy flowing through your body from God.

However, in the National Library of Science, scientific research studies suggest that the physical body has a resonant frequency, which is the natural force of vibration of the body. In another study conducted by Harvard University, researchers found the human body to have a resonant frequency. The resonance frequency is important because it is the measurement of energy in the body that allows the cells to function. The more important question to answer is where did this resonant frequency come from?

Using my understanding of science and the scriptures, the resonant frequency in the body comes from God and functions in the form of energy. Many people of the Christian faith have rejected any teaching involving the word "energy," not realizing the Dunamis power of God flows as active energy, translated as *energeo* in the Greek Dictionary. The active power of God is *energeo,* and on a physical level, the energy flowing through your body from God is the resonant frequency for health.

For by Him, all things were created. Things in heaven and things on earth, things visible and things invisible, all forces of power were created by Him and for Him.
Colossians 1:16 NKJV

Energy is a force of power, and all troops of power were created by God. Energy and power were authored and authorized by God to be used for the greater good of all mankind. Unfortunately, when power gets into the wrong hands, what was meant to be a means of health and livelihood for mankind, becomes an agenda for greed, power, and total control. I don't think God intended for mankind to bankrupt their savings accounts for medical care and medications.

God blew his breath of divine *energeo* into the first man, which has been transferred through all the generations of the original human race. In my study of the scriptures, I found 25 scriptures in the original versions of the New Testament referring to *"energeo"*: *en* – inside and *ergo* – movement. Here are just a few scriptures you can study that demonstrate the various forms of *energeo* that are mentioned in the Bible:

- Mathew 14:2
- Mark 6:14
- Romans 7:5
- 1 Corinthians 12:6
- I Corinthians 12:10
- 1 Corinthians 12:11
- 1 Corinthians 16:9
- 2 Corinthians 1:6
- Galatians 3:5
- Ephesians 1:11
- Ephesians 3:7
- Philippians 2:13

All the cells in your body function based on the exchange of energy within the cells of the body, and if the energy level changes, the cellular function will change. If you are reading this book after the rapture has taken place, you will need to know how to maintain energy levels to sustain healthy functioning for the cells in the body. You must understand who you are and your creation by God to maintain a frequency of healthy survival. This information will be a means of survival during the tribulation when healthcare access comes at the price of relinquishing your freedom to choose.

An Exhortation to the 21st Century Church in America

The 21st Century Church has faltered in accessing everything God created and made by Him and purposed to be used for the Kingdom of God. Because the church has faltered in growing and progressing in the revelation passed on to us from the great generals of faith, we have missed the revelation that comes with seasons shifting and has stagnated in religiosity. This religiosity has caused the church to slowly lose relevancy while fastening to religious patterns that leave the 21st-century Church lifeless and dormant. A lifeless church has come due to a prayerless church, and the prayerless carnal ministry leaders implement strategies for church growth without seeking direction from God through persistent prayer. The 21st-century Church functions through spiritually immature people who have good ideas, but they're not God-inspired ideas because they are generated from prayerless lives. They are too distracted and undisciplined to pray beyond the basic needs of food and safety, and prayerlessness in leadership positions has left the church powerless. And because they refuse to embrace the idea of oneness outside their immediate local church body, they stop the impartation of power from other men and women God from different walks of life with deeper revelation. Instead of the church growing in wisdom and knowledge from impartation from other parts of the Body of Christ, they preach motivational messages to inactive, spoiled, spiritual fat believers who fail to evangelize the message of the gospel.

The prayerless church is packed with people praising God, but they lack the hunger to win souls, and their churches are void of demonstration of the supernatural power of God to clean people up, heal their disease, cast out demons, and raise the dead. The traditional church has become irrelevant and empty while attempting to protect the sacredness of the gospel through structured religious traditions and activities that cause them to circle the mountain every Sunday with no power. While the world uses the knowledge of God's creation to make advancements in technology that advance the kingdom of darkness, the 21st-century church is left in a prayerless and stagnant position, missing important moves of God. For example, while the church was resistant to energy and frequency, understanding God created everything for Him, the world grasps the concepts of God's creation. It is using it in technology to open portals for occult practices to advance the kingdom of darkness.

If the rapture has not happened, we still have time to wake up and rise. We still have time to be a part of the glorified church, with the demonstration of power in preaching the gospel with signs and wonders and actively winning souls before the trumpet sounds. We still have time to repent and recommit to the position of prayer, seeking God with every breath for His direction to share the gospel's message. We still have time to repent from our carnal approaches to grow our churches, which causes us to miss the moves of God that were intended to lead us out of the desert. Because there is still time, we should pray, asking God to give us revelation in His plan for oneness so that we can truly represent the Body of Christ with many members and different functions. We still have time to pray that churches can come together and unite so the 21st-century Church can rise as a bride in glory as one body with one purpose: to share the message of Christ and transform lives with a Kingdom of God mindset.

The Frequency of Faith and Boldness

I expect you remember now how I talked about this when I was with you. You will probably also remember how I used to talk about a "restraining power" which would operate until the time should come for the emergence of this man. Evil is already insidiously at work, but its activities are restricted until what I have called the "restraining power" (of God) is removed.

*When that happens, the lawless man will be plainly seen— though the truth of the Lord Jesus spells his doom, and the radiance of the coming of the Lord Jesus will be his utter destruction. The lawless man is produced by the spirit of evil and armed with all the force, wonders and signs that falsehood can devise. To those involved in this dying world he will come with evil's undiluted power to deceive, for they have refused to love the truth which could have saved them.***2**
Thessalonians 2:5-12 (Phillips)

In a previous chapter, we discussed how the restraining power of the Holy Spirit has been removed from the earth and how the lawlessness that has always existed on earth will now prevail. After the church's rapture, a global EMS broadcast alarm will sound through all cellular devices with a message alerting people of an anomalous phenomenon that resulted in the disappearance of a massive number of people. The message will sound, announcing a global state of emergency, indicating widespread catastrophic events causing utter pandemonium, and will give instructions to remain in your homes for safety.

While the 911 EMS is imploded with calls, people will respond with widespread looting because of fear and desperation for survival in the unknown. The increase of lawlessness and civil unrest will be evident across the globe as a state of emergency requiring the United Nations to assemble to oversee the implementation of a plan for worldwide order and peace for the well-being of all mankind. During this time, known as the tribulation, a world diplomat will arise from the gathering of the United Nations who will have eloquent words and propose an initiative that promises peace starting with the Middle East. This world diplomat will gain much respect and will quickly advance to a position of authority as the anti-Christ. Although the world experiences a short-term peace, it will be short-lived because this diplomat will break promises and become the worst tyrant in the history of all world leaders.

In the initiative for global peace, the plan will involve implementing martial law through military forces of artificial intelligence. The constitutional rights of all civilians will be suspended, subjecting people to searches and inspections with no legal recourse. Similar to the stay-at-home mandate during the COVID-19 pandemic, curfews with stay-at-home orders will be enacted to ensure safety and world order.

Since the freedom of life activities will be curtailed, it will be difficult to freely access some of the life necessities taken for granted, such as healthcare, unless you are having a medical emergency. The days you could go to the urgent care or emergency room with a sore throat and sniffles have ended. Mandates will be implemented through text messaging when you can leave your home for activities of daily living such as grocery shopping, recreation, and medical care unless it's an emergency. If you refuse to abide by the stay-at-home mandates, you will be accused of violating the law for world peace with charges of inciting resistance against the law and order of the United Nations.

After the short term of peace has ended, the anti-Christ system for buying and selling will be fully implemented, requiring a digitalized marking on your hand or forehead with the number 666 attached to your social security number. Although the number 666 will originally be passed off as the new economic system for e-commerce, the primary purpose of the numbers will be revealed during the full implementation, where you will be required to have a marking with a specified deadline. If you do not have a mark by the deadline, you will be locked out of most systems, such as banking, grocery stores, medical systems, restaurants, etc. The 666 will be the symbol marking that identifies you have pledged your allegiance to an anti-Christ system for livelihood and survival that promotes Satanic practices and denies the existence of God.

If you reject the mark of the beast, you will be forced out of the system and will have to quickly learn how to survive by faith by putting your full trust in God for your livelihood. Because all transactions will be processed through a financial system of the anti-Christ, you will be forced from your homes with no means to pay your rent or mortgage. The mark of the beast symbolizing the anti-Christ system will be the infrastructure for the livelihood of all people. It will be the basis of all life activities for transportation, healthcare, employment, banking, and government. If you reject the mark of the beast, you will live in exile of the land, like a sojourner moving from place to place until your time comes to enter eternal glory.

When the anti-Christ is fully implemented, you will not have access to health care and will have to use faith for alternative options for medical care outside of the anti-Christ system. You must trust God to find underground pop-up medical clinics from healthcare professionals who have rejected the mark of the beast and put their faith in God and providing medical care. During the tribulation, pop-up medical clinics will move from city to city to provide medical care for people who do not have the mark of the beast. Most of the healthcare professionals in these clinics will operate as healers who understand the body's biology using wisdom from God's Word. These underground pop-up clinics will open and close quickly and only last briefly. Since providing medical care outside the anti-Christ will be an act of illegal opposition against the one-world order, healthcare providers and patients who seek care at these pop-up clinics will be charged with incitation and sentenced to the judgment of public persecution and death.

Before the rapture, we saw signs of new infrastructure being laid as we witnessed levels of persecution as people lost their jobs because they exercised their freedom of choice in refusing to follow mandates of mass vaccination during the COVID-19 pandemic. Even though some of these people were vindicated and reinstated in their positions of employment with financial retribution, during the tribulation, the persecutions were much more severe and brutal than the world has ever seen, with no recourse or retribution.

During the tribulation, if you refuse the anti-Christ marking and profess the name of Jesus, you will be identified as a "Resistor" against the one-world order for peace. The law for persecution will allow your persecution to be on public display for punishment to instill fear and control over other Resistors who reject the anti-Christ marking and profess Jesus. Similar to the tomes of ancient Rome when people were put on display in a sports arena to fight to their death as a form of entertainment for resisting the law of the land, the persecution of tribulation believers will be bloody and brutally unfair with a primary objective of death through torture.

Similar to battles that were fought in ancient history where one representative was selected to represent the entire group, one tribulation believer will be assigned to lose in a ruthless struggle only to leave other tribulation believers under the hand of a hard taskmaster for persecution through torture. I forewarn you that persecution through torture will be the worst imaginable torture ever in the history of time. When they persecuted Jesus, they beat him with the cat of nine tails that ripped the skin off His body where he was unrecognizable as a man, and the torture was much worse.

Rember the word that I said unto you, the servant is not greater that his lord. If they have persecuted me, they will also persecute you: if they have keep my saying, they will keep yours also.
John 15:20 (KJV)

You Will Need to Live by Faith

During this time, you must live by faith and trust God for your livelihood by understanding the instructions from

God's Word in this book. If you cannot find the underground pop-up clinic with the healer, you must learn how to access the divine energy of God flowing through your body for health and strength. You will need to learn how to use faith in God's Word to access substance from God's Word in an invisible subatomic form.

Now faith is the substance of things hoped for, the evidence of things not seen.
Hebrews 11:1 (NKJV)

You need faith in this very hour that can be termed as "now faith." Now is the time; you must use faith to release the invisible moving substance harnessed in God's Word, which is activated through belief. If you are making a stand for Jesus after the rapture, you are a tribulation believer and will have to learn to live in a way you have never lived before. You have exhausted the time to question and deliberate the concept of faith and whether God's Word really works. If you are a tribulation believer, you must live by faith. So, you muster up your attention and focus on understanding that you will

4 But He answered and said, "It is written, 'Man shall not live by bread alone, but by every word that proceeds from the mouth of God."
Matthew 4:4 (NKJV)

You are living in the very hour of the tribulation that has been prophesied for thousands of years, where you literally must live from God's Word to survive until they find you for persecution. You must quickly learn how to use faith because faith in God's Word will keep you strong when resources are scarce and far between. What you are about to read may sound strange, but God's Word is an active substance with a vibrational frequency. In these trying times, let the vibrancy of God's eternal word illuminate your path, for His truths are everlasting and unfailing, guiding you through darkness into His marvelous light.

12 For the word of God is living and active and full of power [making it operative, energizing, and effective]. It is sharper than any two-edged sword, penetrating as far as the division of the soul and spirit [the completeness of a person], and of both joints and marrow [the deepest parts of our], exposing and judging the very thoughts and intentions of the heart.
Hebrews 4:12 (Amplified)

When you use faith in God's Word, you access an active living power that releases a vibrational frequency. God's Word is a divine substance breathed from the mouth of God that is alive, powerful, and energetic. When you use faith in God's Word and access divine power harnessed in God's Word, your faith becomes the object that carries frequency. You were created in the likeness and image of God: as the Creator's creative being, your faith can release a frequency for what you need for survival. Either you will direct your faith based on the collective consciousness of fear and anxiety that controls the masses using tactics of scarcity and bodily harm, or you will use faith in God's Word and trust God for your livelihood for your appointed time to eternal glory.

To everything, there is a season, and a time to every purpose under the heaven:

You must live by faith and because of your faith you will be hated, oppressed, and forced out of society. You will be the outcast of society and negatively labeled as a "Resistor" because you rejected the mark of the anti-Christ. You will be forced to live in hiding outside of the system of the anti-Christ in remote areas in communities of people who have rejected the mark of the beast. These communities will be similar to the nomads moving from place to place to find an unoccupied remote area to settle and survive until the second coming of Jesus. But there will be two groups of people living within these remote communities, the "resistors" and the "rebels." As previously mentioned, the resistors will be a group of people who refuse the mark of the anti-Christ because they put their faith in God and profess allegiance to Jesus. The "rebels" are a division of the remote communities of people who refuse the mark of the anti-Christ because they revolt against all forms of organized government and religion that pose a threat to the freedom of personal rights and privacy. Although the "resistors" and "rebels" attempt to reside together, there will be constant conflict between the two groups because the resistors live by faith in God's Word for survival.

In contrast, the rebels use uncivilized means of survival by stealing, cheating, and robbery. These remote communities of resistors and rebels will not last long as the insurgents' unlawful activities will disrupt the resistors' lives, requiring a separation into smaller groups and making it more difficult to survive off the land. Subsequently, the one-world government will implement laws stating all remote communities as illegal opposition against the one-world order and sentence residents of remote communities with a judgment of public persecution and death.

You must live by faith and trust God's Word for wisdom to survive off the land until they find you and put you to death. As you believe and live by faith in God's Word, a vibrational frequency of divine substance is released, making your survival possible.

Jesus said to him, "If you can believe, all things are possible to him who believes."
Mark 9:23 (NKJV)

Your belief is critical and makes it possible for all things to live in the hardship of the tribulation. Since you will lose every privilege in society, like scheduling a doctor's appointment and going to the Urgent Care or emergency room, your survival in the tribulation will require you to use faith in God's Word. In the shadows of trials, akin to the Israelites wandering in the wilderness because of their disobedience, they became dependent solely on manna from heaven; your journey, too, is a testament to unwavering faith because you failed to yield to the message of salvation. But just as the early Christians upheld their belief amidst persecution, drawing strength from the Holy Spirit, your reliance on God's Word shall be your beacon and shield. Your survival will be dependent on your faith. It would help if you lived by faith.

11 But that no one is justified by the law in the sight of God is evident, for "the just shall live by faith."
Galatians 3:11 (NKJV)

Although you were left behind from the rapture, if you put your faith in Jesus as your Lord and Savior, you are the "just." They just have to live by pure faith and be strong, and they will not have room to waiver. You must be relentless in your faith because your food will be scarce, and your meals will be rare and far between, requiring you to ration your supply so you grow weak through starvation.

As famine worsens across the globe, you will see an increase in the prevalence of neurological diseases such as prion disease, where people's bodies become stiff with the loss of control over their bodily functions as a result of cannibalism. You will need to use faith against new strains of viruses and diseases that will become more prevalent as people become anthropophagus or people eaters living as savages as a means of survival. You will need to live by faith when traveling in any public arena, as tribulation preachers and believers will become targets for public persecution as the world's hate for Jesus increases through an anti-Christ system. Unfortunately, they flush you out of the system for open display to find all tribulation preachers and believers who will lose their lives refusing to denounce Jesus.

For whosoever will save his life shall lose it: and whosoever will lose his life for my sake shall find it.
Matthew 16:25 (NKJV)

When they find you, they will deliver you to the anti-Christ court system, where you will be hated and sentenced to fight against beastly creatures embodied by demonic spirits. These fights will be brutally unfair and bloody; you must use faith and not lose heart.

There will be no justice for the tribulation preachers and believers; you will not be protected under the constitution of the First Amendment for separation of church and government as the law will be overturned with a final declaration of a one-world religion. As you gather as tribulation preachers and believers during the tribulation, I caution you to use faith to discern the people around you. Many will claim to be with you in your stand against the anti-Christ system but will be sent to flush you out for open display by shapeshifters or Skinwalkers who are demon spirits embodied in flesh bodies that will live among you. They will appear vulnerable and innocent, but they are vicious wolves assigned to deliver you up for slaughter. The world will see evil and lawlessness worse than ever before in the history of time, and your only recourse will be your eternal reward in glory when you die.

It would help if you used faith because you will be tempted to fear as catastrophic events sweep the globe and stars fall from the skies in meteorite showers. The earth's nature you once knew will no longer exist as the ecosystem becomes non-existent from record temperature heat storms that will destroy all forms of vegetation. The blood-red oceans will contaminate all water with toxins, and all drinking water will be unsafe. You must use faith to overcome the doubt and fear as the world continues to deteriorate from God's wrath. If you feel yourself losing heart and doubting in faith, meditate on God's Word in this book and ask God to help you increase your faith and lead you by His wisdom to stand strong in the evil day.

If any of you lack wisdom, let him ask of God, that giveth to all men liberally, and upbraided not; and it shall be given him. 6 But let him ask in faith, nothing wavering. For he that wavered is like a wave of the sea driven with the wind and tossed.
James 1:5-6 (KJV)

Stand Bold in the Armor of God

To use faith and fight successfully, you must stand bold in the armor of God. Before the rapture, many believers failed to understand God equipped them with a suit of armor, and because they failed to use the armor of God, they were wounded by the arrows shot by the enemy, which weakened their faith to stand boldly. Because they were unable to use the discipline to learn about the armor of God, they sat wounded on the sidelines of life, injured by arrows of depression, anger, unforgiveness, carnality, etc.

To stand bold in the tribulation, you must understand that when you accept Jesus Christ as your personal savior, you are equipped with spiritual armor to stand on evil days. You are in that evil day. As a matter of fact, during the tribulation you are in the most evil and darkest times the world has seen, and you have been equipped with spiritual armor to stand. If you are not familiar with the spiritual armor of God, it is found in Ephesians 6:10-18.

The Whole Armor of God

10 Finally, my brethren, be strong in the Lord and in the power of His might. 11 Put on the whole armor of God, that you may be able to stand against the wiles of the devil. 12 For we do not wrestle against flesh and blood, but against principalities, against powers, against the rulers of [b]the darkness of this age, against spiritual hosts of wickedness in the heavenly places. 13 Therefore take up the whole armor of God, that you may be able to withstand in the evil day, and having done all, to stand. 14 Stand therefore, having girded your waist with truth, having put on the breastplate of righteousness, 15 and having shod your feet with the preparation of the gospel of peace; 16 above all, taking the shield of faith with which, you will be able to quench all the fiery darts of the wicked one. 17 And take the helmet of salvation, and the sword of the Spirit, which is the word of God; 18 praying always with all prayer and supplication in the Spirit, being watchful to this end with all perseverance and supplication for all the saints.
Ephesians 6:10-18 (NKJV)

God made sure your suit of armor was custom-made for the current circumstances you are facing the tribulation. You must be diligent in staying aware you are covered by an invisible suit of God's armor that is powered up with your belief. In my book "The Bible-Body

Connection" I talked about using the armor of God to stay healthy; however, during the tribulation, the armor of God must be used as a means of survival in everything you do. You must understand you are wearing armor because the strategies and schemes of the devil will be very sophisticated. They will use advanced technology to produce signs and wonders, so even the very elect of tribulation preachers and believers will be deceived.

They will use technology to lure people with holographic images that will be portals into another dimension of virtual reality but have demons awaiting to ambush you. During the tribulation, you will need an original version of the Bible to discern truth, while the world will believe a lie. The truth of God's Word works like a *belt of truth* supporting your bold and courageous stance. You will not be able to stand in boldness without the *belt of truth* as evil increases and the world grows dark. In the tribulation, you will not be able to blend but must either accept the mark of the anti-Christ or wear the *breastplate of righteousness* that will identify you as the righteousness of God. You will be required to come out from among the world's anti-Christ system and be separated from them. In a dark and oppressed world, you wear *shoes of the gospel,* and you must find peace and comfort to stand in persecution while the wrath of God is being poured out over the globe for rebellion against God. As mentioned earlier, you must really know the scriptures from the Word of God, which is the *shield of faith*. Knowing and understanding the scriptures is your *helmet of salvation* to keep you strong in faith and stand in boldness while demon forces shoot fiery arrows in your thoughts, causing you to doubt the power and goodness of God. You must use the *sword of the Spirit* and wisdom when and how to use the scriptures and rely on the power of the Word harnessed in God's Word to work for you. During this time, you must be a real authentic believer because eloquent speech, charisma, singing abilities, and well-formatted messages won't work. You must be a real, legitimate believer who can skillfully use the Word of God. You must live by faith to be bold and courageous in your position as a tribulation preacher and believer, and your eternal reward will be great.

An Exhortation for the 21st Century Church in America

If you are reading this chapter and the rapture has not occurred, I need to exhort you as the 21st Century Church in what the church is calling "faith." For decades, we have heard messages preached admonishing us with the words "the just shall live by faith" when many of the 21st Century Church lived by the emotions of fear and anxiety, trusting other means for their livelihood. The truth is that people who "just live by faith" will be the tribulation preachers and believers that we ignored and snubbed, who will be left behind and learn to live by faith to survive. They will have to live by faith just to obtain simple necessities to survive, like food and water, when the 21st Century church grumbled in faith about obtaining the Gucci bag, Bently, or million-dollar mansion. The tribulation believer will have to just live by faith when they are forced out of the system to live in remote communities with end-time unstable weather conditions and beastly creatures roaming the earth.

Similar to the restrictions that were placed on people for employment for declining the COVID-19 vaccination during the pandemic, tribulation preachers and believers will not have viable employment with no means of income and will have to live by faith, exchanging work for a meal as a means of survival. At the same time, the 21st-century Church calls it living by faith for money to overindulge in worldly pleasures.

As the 21st Century Church labels their convenient sporadic church attendance and commitment as an act of living by faith, tribulation believers attempt to gather for worship, and they will be forced underground while being hunted by predators carrying a bounty for tribulation preachers and believers to be persecuted to death. Tribulation believers will die for their faith, while the 21st Century Church refuses to live for their faith by daily dying to the pleasures of the flesh that change our commitment to God. To say the least, we make excuses for our lack of commitment from strategic schemes to weaken the commitment of faith and church attendance while enjoying the distractions of life in activities like little league, soccer, cheerleading, family gatherings, festivals, work schedules, etc. e. If major corporations like Wall Street can shut down financial organizations on Sundays, you would think people in the church would make a bold stand of faith. "As for me and my house, on Sundays, we commit to supporting the church in regular church attendance and service. The 21st Century Church, on the whole, does not the "just living by faith," but it is the "just living by the convenience of faith." The real just that live by faith are tribulation preachers and believers who will have to make everyday sacrifices to survive because they missed the rapture and will have to make a stand of faith during the tribulation to advance the Kingdom of God in an evil anti-Christ world.

If the rapture has not occurred yet, we still have time. There is still time left to get it right, be the "just that lives by faith," and make a real stand to live by faith. We still have the opportunity to truly forsake the worldly pleasures that distract us away from church attendance and service to advance the Kingdom of God on earth until Jesus returns. We still have a chance to live by faith and give up the possessions that interfere with our commitment to live by faith with a fully surrendered and committed life to God. Reflect upon the early church, which thrived under the Apostles' guidance, enduring persecution while steadfastly focusing on the spiritual rather than the temporal. Consider the example of Paul, who renounced his worldly status and possessions to pursue a life wholly devoted to Christ. There is still time to set the boundary with the relationships you put before God that watered down your commitment. I encourage you to make the sacrifices to stand boldly in these last days and be the church where they just truly live by faith.

The Frequency of Focus and Mediation

But understand this, that in the last days there will come times of difficulty. For people will be lovers of self, lovers of money, proud, arrogant, abusive, disobedient to their parents, ungrateful, unholy, heartless, unappeasable, slanderous, without self-control, brutal, not loving good, treacherous, reckless, swollen with conceit, lovers of pleasure rather than lovers of God. 2
Timothy 3:1-4 (ESV)

Since the rapture has taken place, one of the most important things you must immediately implement is gaining control over your thoughts and emotions. Especially during the first year after the rapture, the entire earth will be covered with great sorrow. As mass media broadcast worldwide events of mass disappearances of people with stories about missing families, friends, and co-workers, deep grief will sweep across the entire globe, leaving people left behind distraught and seeking answers. Immediately after the rapture, the emergency service system (EMS) will be flooded with calls from panic-stricken people attempting to make missing person reports. Still, due to the mass volume of calls, there will be a recorded message from a system overload.

Emotions of grief and loss will be present everywhere as people use social media to post pictures and stories of their babies and children with the captions "**My Baby was Taken**."

Because the Holy Spirit's presence as the Comforter will be absent from earth, there will be no comfort for grieving people. The grief will be very deep, resulting in excessive use of alcohol, drug use, and sexual immorality as forms of self-medication to escape the deep emotional pain.

Additionally, the great sorrow will increase as people hear nonstop media coverage of worldwide events such as pilots' sudden disappearance from their airplanes while carrying a full cargo of people to a scheduled destination or bus drivers' disappearance with an entire bus full of school-age children. The mass media will broadcast news about train derailments resulting in widespread destruction and death and fatal injuries to laborers as heavy equipment operators suddenly disappear. The sorrow will continue as people who knew the truth about Jesus's return are left with regret because they did not surrender their lives to Jesus and yield to the message of salvation.

You will hear various explanations about people declared missing as an unexplainable electromagnetic frequency that dematerialized physical bodies or an alien invasion abducting people from all over the world. The truth of the rapture will be hidden from the masses left behind. I assure you that your family and friends have not been dematerialized into an unknown abyss or held hostage on an alien ship. Everyone who has been declared missing or taken has something in common: your family, friends, and co-workers all have one thing: they put their faith in Jesus and have been raptured to heaven to be with Jesus. You have entered into a time of the seven-year tribulation where babies and children across the globe have been taken out of the world to escape the wrath of God on people who rebelled against Him. The masses of people across the world who have been reported as missing are not missing at all. They are in heaven with Jesus.

Then we who are alive and remain shall be caught up together with them in the clouds to meet the Lord in the air. And thus we shall always be with the Lord.
1 Thessalonians 4:17 (NKJV)

This scripture will likely be removed from the original version of the Bible because this verse reveals a truth that will be covered and hidden from the masses. As the sorrow and regret intensify, you must understand what has just happened so you can gain control over negative thoughts and emotions that release a frequency that influences the collective consciousness around the globe. More importantly, negative thoughts and emotions release a frequency that affects the little universes in the body called cells.

You must gain control over your thoughts because thoughts carry a frequency that affects chemicals in the body that can cause things to materialize into sickness and disease in the body. Your thoughts literally matter because thoughts release chemical substances of matter in your body that create structures that will either support health or make you defenseless against disease. I understand that asking you to control your thoughts and emotions during mass chaos and confusion can be unrealistic. But, if you don't gain control of your thoughts, your brain will be hijacked by the collective consciousness of stress and anxiety that will result in animalistic-like behaviors for survival. The looting, riots, and civil unrest happening around you are the result of a collective consciousness of fear and anxiety that is sweeping across the globe.

During the worst time in history, especially for people left behind on earth, you will need to quickly gain control over your thoughts and emotions if you plan to stay strong and strategize life in the tribulation. You must gain control over negative emotions because all these feelings of fear, anxiety, anger, guilt, regret, and bitterness affect health, making the body susceptible to sickness and disease. You must immediately gain control over your thoughts and emotions so you can disconnect from the world's collective consciousness and gain wisdom to problem-solve and strategize through difficult times. During the tribulation, you will need to strategize your survival because the persecution of tribulation believers will be worse than the murders of innocent people during the Holocaust.

When you carry intense negative thoughts of panic and anxiety with emotional unrest for too long, it affects the hypothalamus-pituitary-adrenal axis system, triggering hormones to be released that cause inflammation in the body, resulting in disorders such as headaches, depression, memory problems, insomnia, stomach ulcers, high blood pressure, elevated blood sugars, frequent colds, and autoimmune diseases. Since access to public healthcare will not be available without surrendering to an anti-Christ system through an embedded digitalized marking on your right hand or forehead, you will need to take care of yourself and avoid anything that will cause inflammation that precedes just about every disease. To control your thoughts and emotions, you will have to become skillful in the art of meditation. Just as David meditated on the law of the Lord Day and night, finding peace and strength (Psalm 1:2), you too can cultivate a meditative focus that transcends earthly troubles.

This Book of the Law shall not depart from your mouth, but you shall meditate in it day and night, that you may observe to do according to all that is written in it. For then you will make your way prosperous, and then you will have good success.
Joshua 1:8 (NKJV)

To navigate through this evil and dark world, you must become an expert in the art of meditation and practice meditating day and night because your thoughts affect the environment of your body to stay strong and healthy. As in the previous chapter, you are an original creation of God, made with creative power through the breath of God that was blown into the first man, Adam, and transferred down through generations of mankind. You must use that creative power to send a frequency of health into your body to keep your body strong to live in the dark days of tribulation. When not meditating, you must discipline your thoughts to think about things that will create chemicals in your body that support health.

Finally, brethren, whatever things are true, whatever things are noble, whatever things are just, whatever things are pure, whatever things are lovely, whatever things are of good report, if there is any virtue and if there is anything praiseworthy—meditate on these things. 9 The things which you learned and received and heard and saw in me, these do, and the God of peace will be with you.
Philippians 4:8-9 (NKJV)

You must consciously disengage your mind from any negative reports that will cause panic and anxiety. You must practice disciplining the mind to meditate on God's Word for inspiring ideas for daily resources to live by. Prolonged negative thoughts are harmful to your health because these thoughts release hormones that cause inflammation and damage to the inner lining of delicate blood vessels in the arteries around your heart, brain, and kidneys. When these arteries are damaged, it increases the risk of heart disease, stroke, and kidney disease, and you don't want to be sick and at the mercy of an anti-Christ system during the tribulation. In times of trial, recall the steadfastness of Job, who endured great suffering yet never wavered in his faith. Let his perseverance inspire you to cling to the promises of God, for as He was with Job in his trials, so too will He guide and protect those who trust in Him through all adversities.

You must meditate to discipline your thoughts and emotions. Your emotions have resonated frequencies that carry sound waves throughout your body that affect your cells. For example, it is suggested that negative thoughts that emit emotions of fear, grief, guilt, shame, and anger are lower frequencies that can override and scramble the frequency of health of 62-78 megahertz. Although previous studies quantifying emotional frequency were limited, by the time of the rapture, advanced technology will be able to quantify emotional frequency and health, if not already.

God designed the cells in the body to repair and regenerate with emotions of acceptance, peace, joy, and love that carry the highest frequencies. With all the chaos and confusion around you, I want to walk you through a meditation practice for thoughts and emotions of acceptance, peace, joy, and love that foster health and strength. For illustration, I want to briefly refer to the Abraham-Hicks Emotional Vibrational Scale, which does not appear to be a psychometrically validated scientific tool at the time this book is authored but is valuable for introducing a scientific perspective on the laws of attraction by Esther Hicks.

Although the origin of the scale raises questions, the emotional vibrational scale provides valuable insight that can be used in its proper context for health.

The instruction to become an expert at meditation goes beyond the need to raise your vibrational field. The instructions come as a necessity to stay healthy and avoid needing the anti-Christ one-world medical system. You are created in the likeness and image of God, and God made the frequency that comes from thoughts and emotions.

16 For by Him all things were created in heaven and on earth, visible and invisible, whether thrones or dominions or principalities or powers. All things were created through Him and for Him.
Colossians 1:16 (NKJV)

Using the quote from the world-renowned scientist Albert Einstein, *"Everything is energy, and that is all there is to it. Match the frequency of reality you want, and you can't help but to get that reality. It can be no other way."* Numerous scientific research has shown that persistent anxiety, unforgiveness, anger, depression, and resentment have harmful effects on the body that cause inflammation in the body, decreasing immune system functioning. Through the process of deductive reasoning, if everything is energy, including your thoughts and emotions, and energy from thoughts and emotions that flow in the body affect cellular function, we could safely say negative thoughts would have a negative effect on the cells while positive thoughts would have a positive effect on the cells. This could be the main reason why God instructed us to think about good things in Philippians 4:8.

So, using that reasoning, I want to walk you through Transcendental Meditation, which uses mantras for inner peace and staying healthy, except we will replace mantras with God's Word because Joshua 1:8 says the book of the law should not leave your mouth, but you should meditate on it. I want to show you how to develop the discipline to gain control over negative thoughts by meditating on the truth of God's Word so your thoughts vibrate energy to the cells to keep you healthy and strong in the tribulation.

Acceptance

The frequency of acceptance comes as you fully acknowledge the fact that you have been left behind from the rapture, and you release all regret and guilt of your mistake in failing to acknowledge Jesus. Acceptance understands the truth you have been left behind and that you can do nothing to change or undo what has been prophesied for years. You don't have any time to wallow in regret and guilt, but you must make the mental shift to a place of acceptance to release a frequency for health to stay strong through tribulation. Shifting into a mental state of acceptance will allow you to open your mind to creative insights and strategies to flow for your daily survival. Even though you are experiencing emotions of anger, regret, and fear about your future, you must move into acceptance so your body's stress response does not hijack your thought process for creative ideas, concepts, and insights for life in the tribulation.

Since the rapture of the church has impacted the entire globe, you are not alone in your emotions of grief at being left behind without your family and friends. Acceptance is living truth every day and necessary is a process that allows you to move forward and live in the moment of each day, understanding you are not alone because you are accepted as the beloved by

God *to the praise of the glory of His grace, by which He made us accepted in the Beloved.*
Ephesians 1:6 (NKJV)

The following instructions will guide you into a meditation of acceptance.

Find an area where you will not be distracted and sit comfortably with your eyes closed. Take three to five deep breaths to calm the mind, holding the breath for about 3 seconds before exhaling. Sit quietly and take note of any painful emotions or tensions in the body. Don't interpret or allow your mind to be trapped in reasoning. Sit quietly and silently repeat, *"I am accepted by God and receive ideas, concepts, and insights to stay safe, healthy, and strong."*

Peace

Peace is a state of mind with a frequency that also supports health in the physical body.

The peace I am referring to is an internal peace that is deep within the soul and settles the mind to protect the physical body from the harmful effects of stress. In a world of chaos and lawlessness, you will need to make decisions and live by an internal peace that needs to be the ruling factor in your life.

Peace, I leave with you, My peace I give to you; not as the world gives do I give to you. Let not your heart be troubled, neither let it be afraid.
John 14:27 (NKJV)

Reflect on the tranquility that Daniel found in the lion's den, a symbol of divine protection amidst overwhelming peril. His peace was not derived from his surroundings but from a steadfast faith in God's providence. Embrace this deep-seated peace as your shield against the turmoil of the world, for it is through such faith that we are fortified against the storms of life. Peace is a state of mind with a frequency that also supports health in the physical body.

The peace I am referring to is an internal peace that is deep within the soul and settles the mind to protect the physical body from the harmful effects of stress.

You will keep him in perfect peace, whose mind is stayed on You, because he trusts in You.
Isaiah 26:3 (NKJV)

As previously mentioned, during the first year of the rapture, a political leader who will be anti-Christ will rise up and bring peace to the world, but that peace will not last. He will be handsome, charming, witty, with eloquent words and profound answers to problems that bring solutions for world peace. This is not the type of peace I am referring to because the world peace the anti-Christ brings will be temporary, resulting in broken promises and betrayal. The peace I am referring to is a permanent peace that comes from acknowledging Jesus Christ and accepting the love of God. It's a type of peace that passes your understanding when the outer circumstances look grim, and it seems like all hope is lost. It's a type of peace that blankets the soul and helps you stand firm as you face persecution. The kind of peace allowed the three Hebrew men, Shadrach, Meshach, and Abednego, to stand in bold confidence when thrown into the fiery furnace for their faith in God. When King Nebuchadnezzar sentenced the three men to be executed because they refused to bow down to a false god, the King ordered the furnace to be turned up seven times hotter than it was usually heated. It was so hot that the guards assigned to take the three men to their deaths by fire were killed by the heat of the flames. When the three men were thrown into the fire, they found Jesus standing in the fire with them, having no harm without even a scent of smoke on them

(Daniel 3: 10-25). When Stephen, the first Christian martyr in the Bible, was stoned to death for preaching his faith, it was Stephen's peace that gave him the conviction to pray out to God only to fall asleep as his body bled profusely from repetitive blunt force from large stones that were thrown at him during his execution. (Acts 7:51-60) You must enter the peace of God, which will keep you guard your heart and cause your soul to rest during the tribulation.

Be anxious for nothing; but in everything by prayer and supplication with thanksgiving let your requests be made known unto God. And the peace of God, which passes all understanding, shall keep your hearts and minds through Christ Jesus.
Philippians 4:6-7 (NKJV)

This type of peace will be like a military guard over your heart, mind, and soul so you can endure the hardship you will experience. And when you arrive at this state of peace, you must guard your heart from anything that will try and disturb that inner peace. To guard your peace, you must protect your ears and heart from the overload of information coming from the mass media with live news coverage of death and destruction that is designed to incite fear as darkness continues to increase over the earth. You must diligently focus on God, the true author of peace, because the promise of peace from government officials will not last. Nothing in this world will ever be able to duplicate the inner peace that comes from God. The peace of God anchored to your heart will allow you to stand boldly in your faith when they persecute you.

The peace of God is available for every tribulation believer who puts their faith in God when they are publicly tortured to their deaths and put on display for the entire world as a form of sports entertainment. Peace from God will be evident in tribulation to believers who stand in faith and profess Jesus Christ, and this peace cannot be manufactured or reduplicated. As you sit quietly during your meditation, silently repeat, *"I have the peace of God that rests in my soul, and nothing can take God's peace away from me."*

Hope

You might question, how could I dare instruct you to have hope during a time when there is so much grief and chaos? Because hope is a frequency and is necessary if you want to stay strong and healthy. In previous research studies, hope was found to have protective factors against depression, suicide, and hormones in the stress response that prevent inflammation. You might ask, how can anyone experience feelings of hope when the sound of a baby's cry or hearing children's laughter at a park has been stripped from the earth? Where can there be hope when people have to place bars on their windows, bolt their doors, and close the blinds on the window before dusk as a safety measure? The hope that I am referring to is not wishful thinking or resigning to a futile mindset with no plan for the future. But to the contrary, this is hope that will carry you through the tribulation that comes when you put your faith in Jesus. This hope will anchor your faith and understanding; your end destination is with Jesus and your family for a final reunion in the heavenly inheritance with God throughout eternity.

Blessed be the God and Father of our Lord Jesus Christ, who according to His abundant mercy has begotten us again to a living hope through the resurrection of Jesus Christ from the dead to an inheritance incorruptible and undefiled and that does not fade away, reserved in heaven for you, 5 who are kept by the power of God through faith for salvation ready to be revealed in the last time.
1 Peter 1:3-5 (NKJV)

And I heard a loud voice from heaven saying, "Behold, the tabernacle of God is with men, and He will dwell with them, and they shall be His people. God Himself will be with them and be their God.
Revelations 21:3 (NKJV)

The eternal promise underpins our hope, guiding us as a beacon through the darkness of present trials toward the ultimate victory of righteousness. It's hope that comes with confidently knowing there is an end to the evil, and Satan and all his army will be chained in hell throughout eternity.

16 For men indeed swear by the greater, and an oath for confirmation is for them an end of all dispute. 17 Thus God, determining to show more abundantly to the heirs of promise the [a] immutability of His counsel, confirmed it by an oath, 18 that by two immutable things, in which it is impossible for God to lie, we might have strong consolation, who have fled for refuge to lay hold of the hope set before us. 19 This hope we have as an anchor of the soul, both sure and steadfast, and which enters the Presence behind the veil,
Hebrews 6:16-19 (NKJV)

This hope goes deeper than holding positive thoughts because, during the tribulation, you will experience moments of deep despair as you learn about the unimaginable persecution in death by torture that other tribulation believers faced for putting their faith in Jesus and rejecting the anti-Christ. There is hope that is available for you to anchor your soul during your deepest sorrow as you commit to read and understand the promises of God in the Bible. Your hope will prevent you from retreating or surrendering when you hear the screams of torture and you smell a foul scent of rotted blood, feces, and urine, causing a horrible stench in the air. I apologize for the gruesome details in writing this. The persecutions will be worse than your greatest nightmare because every imaginable and unimaginable evil act will be inflicted on tribulation believers across the globe. Absolutely no one will be safe because demons will be unleashed from hell, and demons have no loyalty and follow the commands of their rankings. People will flee to remote areas off the grid to live in rocks and underground shelters in an attempt to escape the evil. Still, they will be caught by demonic beastly predators and taken before the courts for public humiliation and persecution by torture that the world has never seen before.

With all this around you, when the world is so dark and grim, there is hope in Jesus to anchor your soul. Your hope is in knowing that the hand of God is greater than Satan and all his demonic forces, and God is still in control. God sees all and knows all, and Satan's reign on earth is temporary and will come to an end forever. This will all be over, and it will not be quick enough, but soon, God will create a new heaven and earth where you will spend eternity with Him in peace and tranquility. As you sit quietly during your meditation, silently repeat, *"My hope is in God, who reigns now and forevermore."*

Love

Love is the highest frequency for healing, which was demonstrated in God's love for you. While you were still in sin and disobedience, God sent His Son Jesus to die for you so you may be reconciled with Him. God loved you so much that He gave His only son, and if you believe in Him, you will have life everlasting with Him in eternity.

> *But God demonstrates His own love toward us, in that while we were still sinners, Christ died for us.*
> **Romans 5:8 (NKJV)**

Understanding and receiving God's love will be your lifeline that will sustain you through the tribulation. During a time when you will be hated and betrayed by people who will leave the faith, you must understand God loves you. Even though you were left behind, now that you have put your faith in Jesus, God is just to forgive you of all your sins and loves you deeply. As the Psalmist declared, 'Though I walk through the valley of the shadow of death, I will fear no evil: for thou art with me; thy rod and thy staff they comfort me' (Psalm 23:4). This sacred prayer in Psalm reminds us of God's unwavering presence and protection, reinforcing that even in the depths of tribulation, His love remains a shield and sustenance for those who believe.

You are now the aim of God's love, and God must be the only aim of your love. Now that you have received love, during a time of great grief and turmoil, you must love back. You must love God back.

*You shall love the LORD your God with all your heart,
with all your soul, with all your strength, and with all your
mind, and love thy neighbor as thyself.*
Luke 10:27 (NKJV)

Although you are commanded to love your neighbor,
during the tribulation, you may not be able to trust your
neighbor, but you can trust God. To stay healthy and strong
during this grim time, you will need to demonstrate your
love to God with all your heart, soul, and strength and with
all your mind. Unfortunately, I cannot give you a formula
with steps on how to love God, and you will have to
determine that in your personal relationship with God as you
seek Him on a moment-by-moment basis to guide you in
every move you make during the tribulation.

Interestingly enough, there were many people who were
raptured into heaven because they put their faith in Jesus,
but they never developed a personal relationship with God
because they only had a Sunday relationship with Him.
Although they put their faith in God and made it to heaven
because they had no personal relationship with God, they
will have to spend eternity in heaven but in the outer courts.
They never realized the importance of talking to God on a
consistent basis, yielding to the moment-by-moment
instructions to share Jesus and save a life.

Unfortunately, you do not have that opportunity. You
must live by the moment-by-moment instructions from God
to save your life because they hate God, and they will hate
you. As a tribulation preacher or believer, things will be
extremely difficult for you, and you will need to be in
constant communion with God, or you will simply not make
it to standing for Jesus at this hour. The deep love you have

for God through a personal relationship will allow you to stand bold in confidence in the face of slow, tortuous persecution purposed to wear you down and surrender.

So do not throw away your confidence; it will be richly rewarded.
Hebrews 10:35 (NIV)

Who shall separate us from the love of Christ? Shall tribulation, or distress, or persecution, or famine, or nakedness, or peril, or sword? 36 As it is written: "For Your sake we are killed all day long; We are accounted as sheep for the slaughter." 37 Yet in all these things we are more than conquerors through Him who loved us. 38 For I am persuaded that neither death nor life, nor angels nor principalities nor powers, nor things present nor things to come, 39 nor height nor depth, nor any other created thing, shall be able to separate us from the love of God which is in Christ Jesus our Lord.
Romans 8:35-39 (NKJV)

As you enter your time of meditation, silently repeat *"My heart is persuaded in the love of God, and nothing shall separate me from His love for me and my love for Him."*

Exhortation to the 21st Century Church in America

To the 21st-century Church, if the rapture hasn't happened yet, you don't have any more time to waste in an undisciplined lifestyle. You must choose who you will serve. The days of straddling the fence are over. The days are over for attending a Saturday concert by your favorite artist that promotes the kingdom of darkness with songs and symbolism. Then, think you can sing with the anointing of God on Sunday. Satan made a change in strategy with an open display to promote an agenda of darkness through the music industry and has been using music artists to open portals to allow demons to come and attach to concertgoers to gain access into their homes and churches. God's principles for separation and sanctification were not given to restrict churchgoers but to protect them. You have to decide if you will serve God or enjoy the pleasures of the god they serve. It's time to make a clear choice: It's either God or your favorite secular artist. If you choose not to make a choice, you have been chosen by the prince of darkness by default. There are only two kingdoms: the kingdom of light and the kingdom of darkness; this is the season to choose because the times have shifted, and with every shift, God moves.

In these last days on earth, God is moving through people who are willing to set themselves apart from the world. The time is over for the excuses that God understands your struggle to choose world idols for pleasure over Him. Yes, God understands and will always love you, but your carnal, disobedient lifestyle will cut off the blessings of the Abrahamic covenant that comes with alignment and obedience. Suppose you are out of alignment, living a compromised lifestyle but still experiencing rewards, fame, and notoriety. In that case, it may be coming from evil forces with a strategic plan to bring reproach to representatives of the kingdom of God.

You can no longer comprise your walk as a servant of God. You must choose whether you will be a faithful or unfaithful servant. The loyal servant uses time wisely, curtailing any activity that doesn't relate to advancing the kingdom of light. The faithful servant is mindful that time is short and focuses on daily activities that will find them in the kingdom of light business when Jesus returns. When Jesus returns unexpectedly, what will He find you doing?

Will you be found sitting in a park on a warm Sunday at a Jazz Festival or sitting in church to get equipped for the fight during these last days? Will you be found at a world tour concert of your favorite secular artist, or will you be found fellowshipping with a body of believers during a Wednesday night Bible study? Will you be found cursing someone out in the store or at work, or will you be found sharing the message of Jesus with them? The time is short, and I encourage the 21st Century Church to get on your post, get in assignment, and be about the Father's business, so when Jesus returns, He finds you as a faithful servant and grants you to be ruler over much. You don't want to be the unfaithful servant that wastes time with unused giftings that will be appointed to the groups of hypocrites where you will live in the outer courts of heaven away from the glory of God. You don't want to stand before God with regrets and excuses, wishing you would have taken advantage of the time of earth to serve God with your time and gifts. You still have time, so get busy.

The Frequency of Declaration

During the time of tribulation, you must declare God's word for health and safety over your body and in your environment. If there is any chance you make it through the tribulation, escaping the tortuous persecutions as contracts will be placed on all tribulation believers, your survival will be weighed heavily by what you say.

Death and life are in the power of the tongue,
And those who love it will eat its fruit.
Proverbs 18:21 (NKJV)

Therefore, I say to you, whatever things you ask when you pray, believe that you receive them, and you will have them.
Mark 11:24 (NKJV)

You will have what you say, so you will need to say what you want and not what you see. This will be a very difficult task since the world will be covered with darkness, and the Word of the Lord will be rare as false prophets take the forefront to deceive people from coming to Christ during the tribulation. Remember the resilience of Elijah, who, in the time of great drought and apostasy, boldly confronted the prophets of Baal on Mount Carmel. Let this story embolden you to stand firm in faith, proclaiming God's truth, even as darkness seeks to obscure it. You will have to learn to encourage yourself in the Word and feed yourself the Word of God continuously to keep your faith strong so you can endure the hard times. The time is up for the church on earth, and the opportunity has ended in going to church to be edified, exhorted, and empowered.

During the tribulation, underground pop-up churches will be led by tribulation preachers sharing messages of strength and hope for tribulation believers who are standing and professing their faith in Jesus. But their churches will be outlawed, and preachers will be hunted down like sheep prey by beastly creatures with an assignment and find tribulation preachers as a sport, and their bodies will be stuffed as trophies of reward. Since there will be a bounty placed on all believers, you must be wise to who is around you.

12 And we urge you, brethren, to recognize those who labor among you, and are over you in the Lord and admonish you,
1 Thessalonians 5:12 (NKJV)

You are living in a time when demon spirits unleashed from hell are authorized to have free reign, and you must have discernment of who is around you. Hebrews 13:2 says, "Do not forget to be friendly and generous to strangers, because some people have entertained angels without even knowing it?" Before the tribulation, angels moved freely throughout the earth on assignment to shift into human form to serve believers. Since the rapture of the church, angelic beings have been removed from the earth, and Satan and his demons have free reign to transform into humans, so you must have discernment. In the tribulation, demon spirits will be camouflaged as Skinwalkers to enter your camps and sit in your underground churches to expose you and offer you up to the courts for the sentencing of torture and death.

Before the rapture, church attendance was not considered a high priority but a Sunday convenience for most believers who will spend eternity in the outer courts of heaven because they failed to understand the value and importance of the church in building a daily relationship with God and his people. As a tribulation believer, you must strategize and use wisdom to stay encouraged in the Lord because persecution awaits you, so you must be wise.

16 "Behold, I send you out as sheep in the midst of wolves. Therefore, be wise as serpents and harmless as doves.
Matthew 10:16 (NKJV)

Before the church was raptured from the earth, the church was a very unique social network as people gathered as believers to connect in faith and worship the Creator God. During these gatherings, many people were healed and empowered with strength. As people in the church gathered as a church body in agreement, the songs of praise and words of declaration released an energy and frequency that changed molecules in the environment and hormones in the body, making all things possible for health and life. As we made declarations using the Word of God, the sound of agreement released a vibrational frequency that opened a portal, allowing blessings to flow to meet the needs of the people. Before the rapture, when believers gathered and released a sound of agreement through decreeing God's Word, they were unaware of the divine portals that were opened from the sound of faith.

During the tribulation, other portals will be open, but they will not be opened by the faith of church believers but presented as holograms with a hole in another dimension. These holograms will be the portal into other dimensions where demons will be waiting for you to ambush you. You must walk in wisdom and avoid the outer appearance of harmless and inviting things. Evil will continue to increase because you live in an evil, dark world.

Remember this one thing: keep God's Word deep within your heart. As previously mentioned, God's word is alive with active breathing power, carrying subatomic invisible substances breathed from the mouth of God and penned by man on ink and paper.

Understand when you speak God's Word, you release a frequency of divine power that is harnessed in the Word of God and will never become extinct or be exterminated.

Your word is settled in heaven. 90 Your faithfulness endures to all generations;

*You established the earth, and it abides. 91 They continue this day according to Your ordinances, For all are Your servants. **Psalms 119:89-91***

The grass withers, the flower fades, But the word of our God stands forever."
Isaiah 40:8 (NKJV)

When you speak God's Word, you release an invisible substance that affects your environment and sends a frequency of health to keep your body strong when food and water are scarce. When you speak God's Word, your words release a frequency that can create a force of energy that can raise your body frequency by 25 megahertz.

God is the divine source of all creation, and when God made this world, everything was made by Him from energy. After God created the world, he created Adam and said let man have dominion. As Adam began to declare names over

God's creation, the animals manifested in the nature of their name because we live in a voice-activated world. Everything existing on earth was created with the sustenance from God the Creator that carries a vibrational frequency and responds to sound and frequency. Everything in existence vibrates with a frequency.

"For you shall go out with joy and be led out with peace; The mountains and the hills Shall break forth into singing before you, And all the trees of the field shall clap their hands.
Isaiah 55:12 (NKJV)

For we know that the whole creation groans and labors with birth pangs together until now.
Romans 8:22 (NKJV)

But He answered and said to them, "I tell you that if these should keep silent, the stones would immediately cry out."
Luke 19:14 (NKJV)

The earth is alive, and everything on it carries a frequency from the Divine Creator God.

After God made the earth, He gave man a divine sanction to subdue the earth: take charge and dominion over every living thing that moves on the planet. Although the real understanding of the dominion God gave man to take charge over all living creation was never understood in the fullest by the raptured church, others valued God's creation and used their understanding of energy and frequency to develop advancements in technology such as drones, solar energy, energy powered flying cars, and innovative medical treatment for cancer and other diseases. Unfortunately, with every positive value, there is a negative value as men used the creation of energy and frequency for personal gain, power, greed, and control, creating a world of technology to gain the world's wealth and riches while subjecting others to hardships through an economic system for daily survival. With every good creative value energy and frequency was purposed to bring, there is an evil purpose to deceive and destroy. The highest point of this evil purpose will be displayed during the tribulation when the false prophet arises during the tribulation and deceives masses of people through signs and wonders that will come from the powers of darkness through Satan himself.

For false Christ's and false prophets will rise and show great signs and wonders to deceive, if possible, even the elect.
Matthew 24:24(NKJV)shape

Beloved, do not believe every spirit, but test the spirits, whether they are of God, because many false prophets have gone out into the world.
1 John 4:9 (NKJV)

11 Then many false prophets will rise up and deceive many. ***Matthew 24:11 (NKJV)***

During the tribulation, there will be many false prophets teaching among the tribulation believers to deceive you from walking in the truth. They will know the Word of God and be cunning in twisting the truth so that you believe the lie. At this time, there will be many false prophets, but there will be one false prophet who will be elevated to a high political position and mesmerize the masses with his power over natural and spiritual elements. This one false prophet will work in participation of a triune network of the anti-Christ, the false prophet, and Satan to create an idol image that blasphemes God and will attempt to destroy the government of God.

You will not have the convenience to pull out your cellular device to look up scriptures. You must know God's Word, meditate day and night, and then speak God's Word over your body to keep the frequency of health at 62-78 megahertz. Don't underestimate God's creation of your body and how your words release a frequency that affects your health. Many believers that have been raptured never ever grasped the concept of the power released from words spoken and lived defeated lives while they were on earth. Proverbs 18:21 says death and life are in the power of the tongue, and a scientist named Dr. Masaru Emoto quantified that scripture with an experiment called the Water Experiment. In a nutshell, the experiment involved using different types of water with specific words and emotions spoken over the water. After the water was frozen and the water crystals were viewed under a microscope, the findings reported that words spoken like hate and anger formed ugly malformed crystals from clean natural spring water, and words spoken like love and joy formed beautiful crystal structures from dirty swamp water. The experience quantified in Proverbs 18:21 is that human speech has dramatic effects on water molecules for life or death in the body.

During a time when you will experience extreme hardship and be forced out of an anti-Christ mainstream society, you will have to develop the discipline to guard the words coming out of your mouth. This is not a spiritual metaphor but is meant to be taken in a literal context. The extent of life and death will be determined by the words you speak because your words have a direct effect on the biology of your body, and your words carry a frequency of vibrations. The indirect effect of negative words carries a frequency that signals the brain to cause the salivary glands to produce cortisol and the adrenals to decrease the production of Oxytocin. When the body has abnormal levels of either one of these two hormones, the body can experience harmful effects. The frequency of health to stay strong and endure till the end is in your mouth as you declare God's Word.

Exhortation of the 21st Century Church in America

To the 21st-century Church, we are stronger together than separated. There is power in unity that creates an atmosphere where anything and all things are possible. The kingdom of darkness is an orderly system that works through rankings of demons in principalities, powers, rulers of the darkness, and spiritual hosts of wickedness. My question is, how is it that Satan and his camp of demons can operate in the order of a ranking system, but the church cannot unite to operate under the ranking system of the body of Christ, understanding there are many members with different tasks? The 21st-century Church has failed to honor and discern the entire body because the infrastructure of the religious organization chooses to associate with people who are only like them. They select people to preach as they preach, dress as they dress, and sing as they sing, and only engage you to be a part of their church just to fill up their building and event venues.

The 21st-century Church has failed to discern the diversities of gifts in the body of Christ as a collective body. I believe God's original plan was that churches all over unite, understanding that one part of the body doesn't have it all, regardless of the size of your church. Although the egos in the leadership of the 21st Century Church would like to think they have the sum total of what the parishioners need, God did not design the body to function separately from its other members. The church has been weak because they fail to discern the other members of the Body of Christ and unite. The 21st-century Church has a sickly appearance because leaders would rather focus on criticizing the diversity of the church rather than embrace the diversity of gifts.

Let me make this clear because I am not referring to a diversity of doctrines with destructive heresies or philosophies presented by false prophets. We have been warned about the last days where false prophets will arise and deceive many people. We are in those days as false prophets condone lifestyles that God has called sin by twisting the truth from God's creating gray areas of argument to turn people's ears from the truth. We are in a time when preachers will operate as false prophets because they teach from the perspective of fulfilling and satisfying the breaches in their souls from past hurt. I don't believe every false prophet was raised to be a false prophet, but it was their ego and lack of accountability to the wisdom of a multitude of counsel that became the fuel that led them into heresy. When spiritual leaders fail to work things out in their own souls, they will use God's Word to intellectualize their sin, treading on the breeding ground of a false prophet. To identify the false prophet in these last days, you must diligently study and know God's Word for yourself. To recognize the false prophet, you must be able to discern the frequency of truth from the frequency of a lie.

In chemistry, polar molecules will be attracted to other polar molecules that are alike.

Similar to the chemistry of polar molecules, if you release a frequency of polar molecules from unresolved pain, you will be attracted to a false prophet with those polar molecules that twist the Word of God to intellectualize their unresolved pain. In these last days, you must know God's Word for yourself. You must study to rightfully divine the word of truth that you are studying and hearing. Then open your mouth and speak the truth in love. Speak the truth that will release a frequency of health that will bring health to your spirit, soul, and body and affect the environment of others around you.

The Frequency of the Covenant Meal

As the tribulation progresses, famine will sweep across the globe, and widespread food shortages will affect every social class. The food shortages will occur as a result of ecological weather changes from cosmic storms and record heat temperatures that will destroy all natural food sources and contaminate the water with toxins. The time will come when you will not be able to go to Walmart, Kroger, Whole Foods, or your favorite grocery store to purchase food.

The food shortage will eventually require all food to be rationed from food storehouses that are structured to be controlled by state and county divisions of the One-World Government. In order for people to qualify to be a recipient of government-issued food, they must have a digitalized mark of the anti-Christ embedded on their right hand or forehead. Without the mark of the anti-Christ, people will not be able to buy food and eventually be forced out of mainstream society. The food distribution lines will be packed with people from every walk of life, with well-known celebrities standing in food lines along with those who were previously known as welfare recipients. During the tribulation, people of higher socioeconomic classes who were always afforded rights and privileges to resources will eventually no longer be regarded based on income, and everyone will be forced to receive the mark of the anti-Christ, or they will be denied access to food or to buy and sell any goods.

He causes all, both small and great, rich and poor, free and slave, to receive a mark on their right hand or on their foreheads, 17 and that no one may buy or sell except one who has the mark or the name of the beast, or the number

Food and Water

If you make it past the first year of the tribulation, you will need to use wisdom to strategize your food and water because, at some point, all-natural sources of food and water harvested from the ground will not be safe to eat. All sources of water, including the ocean, lakes, and streams, will turn blood red and be infused with harmful toxins. The bottled water that was once a convenient part of daily life before the rapture will be scarce, and the increase in food prices will cost half of the day's earnings for one meal per person.

While the world is in panic, you must plan your strategy for how you will survive because darkness will prevail, and every evil work will cover the earth. During the first year of the tribulation, you must use every waking moment of the day to strategize your survival. Remember, shortly after the rapture, people will experience a sense of calmness because all civil unrest will cease, and a One-World government will take action to restructure society with a plan to bring peace, law, and order. Again, do not be deceived by this false sense of peace because it will be brief and is the calm before the worst storm you have ever experienced.

If you make the choice to put your faith in Jesus, you will have to make a bold stand for Jesus that will come at the risk of losing your life. During the tribulation, you will not be able to work the system for resources, but you will be provided the opportunity to make an informed decision to reject God for an anti-Christ or stand in faith and put your trust in God. You will not be able to swindle or con the system by receiving the mark of the anti-Christ on your hand or forehead to become a recipient of government resources because the anti-Christ marking is not only a mark embedded on your hand or your forehead, but it places an eternal mark on the soul symbolizing your choice to reject Jesus. Before the rapture, when people made the decision to put their trust in God and accept the gift of salvation, their choice to accept Jesus was recorded in the Book of Life instituted in heaven. Now that the rapture has taken place, your choice to accept Jesus will be known in the heavens in your choice to reject the anti-Christ marking on your soul. There will be no middle ground or a grey area, but you will be forced to decide if you will trust an anti-Christ system or if you will trust God and suffer the persecution as a tribulation believer.

After a few months into the tribulation, as people begin to process the shock and disbelief as a result of the rapture, you want to identify any thoughts and activities that engage you in the idea of normalcy and rebuilding. There will be no normalcy but complete chaos and utter confusion. As you make the decision to reject the ant-Christ and serve God, your life on earth is temporary, and your mindset must change to that of a sojourner passing through to an eternal destination in glory.

14 Whereas ye know not what shall be on the morrow. For what is your life? It is even a vapor, that appeared for a little time, and then vanishes away.
James 4:14 (KJV)

This is not the time to recover and rebuild, and this is the most important time to strategize your survival left behind in a world where evil will prevail and grow rampant across the globe. You must seize every opportunity to gather resources to prepare for the most evil and dark times the world has ever experienced in the history of time. As God's wrath is released over the earth, severe ecological changes from diverse weather patterns will cause the earth's surface and water to be contaminated with toxins. Any water and food harvested from the ground will be highly toxic and will not be fit for human consumption. At some point, eating healthy and choosing foods "close to the earth" will no longer be recommended. All natural forms of food, including chicken, fish, and beef, will no longer be available except for food that has been cultivated in the laboratory. If vitamins and minerals have not been regulated by the FDA, it will be difficult to purchase them.

11 And great earthquakes shall be in divers' places, and famines, and pestilences; and fearful sights and great signs shall there be from heaven.
Luke 21:11 (NKJ)

During the tribulation, there will be diverse weather patterns with extreme oceanic and atmospheric changes that will affect the ecosystem for all food sources for life. A global famine will cause extreme food shortages, resulting in a limited supply of food. Unfortunately, the severe food shortage will cause people to resort to behaviors of cannibalism, like in the Bible story found in 2 Kings 6:24-30 where two mothers agreed to eat their babies as a way of survival. These dire times echoed through history serve as somber reminders of humanity's limits when faced with extreme scarcity. In these moments, steadfast hope and reliance on God's provision are paramount, reflecting the need to trust in divine sustenance amidst calamity.

People who resort to cannibalism during the tribulation will develop noticeable zombie-type features such as body stiffness, difficulty walking with gait changes, confusion, and difficulty speaking.

While a global food shortage sweeps across the earth, sickness and disease will be widespread as new strains of viruses cause unending pandemics. If you make the choice to put your faith in God, medications and healthcare will not be accessible to you. In a life-threatening emergency, if you do not have the mark of the anti-Christ when you are scanned, you will be left by EMS personnel to fend for yourself and will have to learn to self-treat with herbs and other remedies because you will not have access to the medical system. Similar to the restrictions that were enforced in some countries during the COVID pandemic, a schedule will be provided for people indicating when they are permitted to leave their homes for domestic reasons. Everyone will be required to carry a digital passport similar to the vaccine passport that was developed before the outbreak of the COVID-19 pandemic. The digital regions you are permitted to travel to, and if you attempt to travel outside your designated area, you will be tracked down and arrested. Some pandemics will be skin diseases that will cause hideous-looking sores on the body, but those diseases will be reserved for those who carry the mark of the anti-Christ.

So, the first went and poured out his bowl upon the earth, and a foul and loathsome sore came upon the men who had the mark of the beast and those who worshiped his image.
Revelations 16:2 (NKJV)

You will need to stock up on food resources while you can. Your food selections will be scarce, but it is critically important because certain foods can work like medicine for the body because 70-80% of your immune system is in your stomach and intestines. So, it will be important to secure food with higher frequencies that will support your immune system. You're eating habits must change drastically because mealtime will no longer be a form of recreation but a means of survival. Using this concept that health in the body is sustained at a frequency of 62-78 megahertz, you will need to find food sources to support the frequency of health. You may not know this, but food has a frequency, and there are some foods that have high frequency, and there are foods with zero frequency. Some examples of foods that have zero frequency include processed foods, refined sugar, bleached flour, genetically modified foods, canned fruits and vegetables, frozen pizza and soup, cooked sausages and meats, and pasteurized milk.

In the tribulation, the anti-Christ system will be implemented early, and people's activities will be regulated by a schedule that permits people to leave their homes for activities for daily living. If you reject the anti-Christ markings, you will be prevented from buying any food, water, and miscellaneous items for daily living. Use your time wisely at the beginning of the tribulation, dry-freeze your foods, and pack them away. Dry freeze all nonperishable foods like sun-ripened dried fruits and vegetables, hazelnuts, peanuts, sunflower seeds, dried coconut, almonds, and legumes. During the tribulation, cultivate a self-sustaining garden with seeds of essential crops like wheat, barley, and root vegetables, which can thrive in varied climates. Store medicinal herbs and knowledge of natural remedies, as access to healthcare may be restricted. Prepare secure caches in hidden locations to ensure that your provisions are safeguarded when you are displaced. At some point, you will be evicted from your home, so you must store your food to pack up and go.

The Covenant Meal

The disease will be rampant in the tribulation, and a worldwide famine will result in malnourishment and starvation, affecting people across the globe. Food and water shortages that were once limited to impoverished countries will be prevalent across the globe, resulting in malnourishment and weakened immune systems, increasing the vulnerability to the ongoing epidemics that cause sickness and death. As the tribulation progresses, the warehouses with government-issued food programs will be affected by the global food shortage, forcing the closure of all government-funded food distribution programs. While people trusted the promise of livelihood and well-being offered through an anti-Christ system, they will be left feeling duped and deceived for listening to the lie and accepting the mark of the beast. In reality, no one was duped, but their choice to receive the mark of the beast was a decision made of willful ignorance to reject the message of Jesus.

As the food shortages peak, resulting in utter panic, I want to explain to you a means of survival through a covenant meal called the Lord's Supper, sometimes referred to as Holy Communion. The historical roots of the Covenant Meal trace back to the Passover Meal found in Exodus chapters 7–12 at the time when the Israelites were being held captive as slaves in Egypt, and the people cried out to God for help. God heard the cries of the people and called a man named Moses to deliver them so His people could freely worship Him. But when Pharoh refused to yield to Moses's requests to let the Israelites go, God outstretched His mighty hand in judgment until Pharoh was willing to let God's people go. The first nine judgments were released in plagues that involved the water turning to blood, an infestation of frogs, lice, flies, diseased livestock, boils, hail, locusts, and then the plague of utter darkness that covered the entire region with light-only in the region where the Israelites resided.

As Pharoh's heart hardened at the request from Moses to let God's people go, the final plague involved a death angel that passed through the city with an assignment to kill the firstborn child of every household. God gave specific instructions to Moses' Israelite people to protect their household from the death angel with instructions. Moses was instructed to tell the Israelites to choose a lamb for sacrifice with no defects, one lamb for each household. They were to take special care of the lamb until the 14th day, slaughter the lamb at twilight, take some of the blood of the lamb, and smear it on the sides and top of the doorframes of the houses where they ate the animal. They were to roast the meat over a fire and eat it along with bitter salad greens and bread made without yeast and then burn the leftovers. And on the night of the last plague when judgment was executed against Egypt and their false Gods, when the angel of death saw the blood on the doorposts and passed over them, and the plague of death did not touch because of the blood of a perfect lamb. Since that time, during the Jewish Holiday, the Passover Seder Meal has been a ritual feast to remember the exit of God's people from Egypt.

Now, let's discuss the crucifixion of Jesus and the offering of the perfect lamb without spot or blemish for the remission of sins and eternal life. After God created the earth, He created man in His image for fellowship through man's choice and free will. After the creation of man, God gave man the title deed of the earth, which was referred to as dominion.

26 Then God said, "Let Us make man in Our image, according to Our likeness; let them have dominion over the fish of the sea, over the birds of the air, and over the cattle, over [a] all the earth and over every creeping thing that creeps on the earth."
Genesis 1:26 (NKJV)

At that time, man walked with God in the cool of the day and fellowshipped directly with God on a daily basis. A man had complete dominion over all creation, but there was a serpent that was cunning and tricky, maybe because Satan had embodied the serpent. Satan was an archangel who held a high-ranking position in the kingdom of Light until he was ejected from his position for trying to create a revolt and rebel against God to exalt his own kingdom. At the very moment the thought was conceived, Satan, along with all his angelic followers, fell from heaven. Since that time, Satan and his regime have greatly despised God with the ultimate plan to steal, kill, and destroy all of God's creation, including mankind.

One day, a cunning serpent struck up a conversation with Eve and began to inject thoughts into her mind that caused her to question God and explore knowledge outside God's instruction. The ultimate plan of the serpent was to influence Eve to rebel against the instruction of God, sin and disobey God, and eat the fruit from the forbidden tree of knowledge. After Eve ate the fruit, she gave it to Adam.

So when the woman saw that the tree was good for food, that it was [a]pleasant to the eyes, and a tree desirable to make one wise, she took of its fruit and ate. She also gave to her husband with her, and he ate. 7 Then the eyes of both of them were opened, and they knew that they were naked; and they sewed fig leaves together and made themselves [b]coverings.

8 And they heard the [c]sound of the LORD God walking in the garden in the [d]cool of the day, and Adam and his wife hid themselves from the presence of the LORD God among the trees of the garden.
Genesis 3:6-8 (NKJV)

And because of the sin of Adam's disobedience, mankind lost the title deed with dominion over all the earth. The first Adam lost the title deed, requiring a sinless man to recover the title deed of dominion and bring it back to mankind. Through the virgin birth of Mary, God sent Jesus as a second Adam to become a sacrificial lamb without spot or blemish to be offered as a sacrifice for the remission of sin, restoring mankind back to the position of authority. When Jesus died on the cross, He represented the Lamb of God, who was the perfect blood sacrifice for the remission of sin.

Not with the blood of goats and calves, but with His own blood, He entered the Most Holy Place once for all, having obtained eternal redemption.
Hebrews 9:12 (NKJV)

Jesus became the willing sacrifice to redeem man of sin and back into a position of dominion with authority through Jesus Christ. Because Jesus humbled Himself and removed His heavenly robe of glory, subjected Himself to a horrible beating of 39 stripes with a cat of nine tails, and then willing laid His body down to be nailed on an old wooden cross only to be humiliated through crucifixion, we have remission of sins, eternal life, with covenant promises stamped with the blood of Jesus. In fulfilling ancient prophecies, Jesus' sacrifice correlates directly with the Passover lamb, which was slain to spare the Israelites in Egypt from the final plague. As the ultimate Passover Lamb, Jesus' blood marks the doorposts of our hearts, ensuring our deliverance from eternal death. His resurrection on the third day sealed the new covenant, offering hope and the promise of eternal communion with God.

On the night before Jesus's crucifixion, Jesus hosted a commemorative meal with His disciples called the Last Supper. During this last supper, Jesus gave the disciples instructions during the meal, saying, "Do this in remembrance of me."

For I tell you that from now on, I will not drink of the fruit of the vine until the kingdom of God comes." 19 And he took bread, and when he had given thanks, he broke it and gave it to them, saying, "This is my body, which is given for you. Do this in remembrance of me." 20 And likewise the cup after they had eaten, saying, "This cup that is poured out for you is the new covenant in my blood.
Luke 22:18-20 (ESV)

Communion is a holy meal that we must take as a reminder of Jesus' bruised body and shed blood. The Last

Supper, also known as Holy Communion, reminds us of the persecution Jesus endured by the religious and political leaders when he was tied to a whipping post and whipped with a cat of nine tails, ripping muscle from his bone. It's a holy meal that reminds us that after they beat Him to the point, He no longer looked like a man and that Jesus willingly laid down on the cross and allowed soldiers to nail his hands and feet to a wooden cross where they hung Him in public view to be mocked and humiliated. We are to remember as Jesus hung on that wooden cross, his body experienced extreme pain from complicated lacerations, swelling in his tissues, extreme dehydration, and an inability to reposition His body on the cross to deep breath or sigh. While Jesus hung on the cross, every sin and sickness was transferred onto His body. When He had completed the assignment, He was sent to do it. He spoke, "It is finished," released His Spirit, hung his head and died. Holy Communion is a meal of remembrance and understanding because God loves you. He sent Jesus to earth to be crucified so that you may experience eternal life with God when life on earth is over.

16 For God so loved the world that He gave His only begotten Son, that whoever believes in Him should not perish but have everlasting life.
John 3:16 (NKJV)

The covenant meal includes two elements: a small piece of bread representing the body of Jesus and a small amount of juice or wine that is consecrated to represent the blood of Jesus. It is considered a sacred meal that should be handled with respect and honor and should start with an examination of your heart, searching for thoughts or behaviors unpleasing to God with a heartfelt desire to make the changes for a life surrendered and pleasing to God.

As mentioned earlier, in the beginning months of the tribulation, the original version of the Bible and other translations of the original version will be removed from circulation, and shortly thereafter, Satan will present his plan through the anti-Christ and the false prophet. During the global famine, the anti-Christ will implement a plan to resolve world hunger and bring peace, but their plan will involve using a digitized system of the mark of the beast on the hand or forehead. Force people to receive government assistance for their basic food needs. If you refuse the mark of the beast on your hand or forehead, you will not be able to buy or sell and will not have access to food and water.

Since you will not have access to regular meals, you must partake in the covenant meal on a daily basis and remember you have covenant promises with God. Although many tribulation believers and preachers will be publicly persecuted and put to death, the covenant meal will keep you in remembrance there is eternal life awaiting you when your life ends on earth. During the tribulation, set aside time every day to remember Jesus paid the ultimate sacrifice for your life through the shedding of His blood for the remission of your sins and eternal life with Jesus and your family and friends in heaven. Reflect upon the early church's practice of breaking bread together in Acts 2:46, where believers met daily to share in the Lord's Supper, reinforcing their unity and commitment to faith despite persecution. Just as they drew strength from these acts of remembrance, so too should you find solace and sustenance in your daily observance of the covenant meal throughout the tribulation. Grab a small piece of food and use it as a symbol of Jesus' body. Then, take a small amount of any beverage and use it as a symbol of Jesus' blood. Declare your covenant rights for protection and preservation until the second rapture.

Then Jesus said unto them, Verily, verily, I say unto you, Except ye eat the flesh of the Son of man, and drink his blood, ye have no life in you. 54 Whoso eateth my flesh, and drinketh my blood, hath eternal life; and I will raise him up at the last day. 55 For my flesh is meat indeed, and my blood is drink indeed. 56 He that eateth my flesh, and drinketh my blood, dwelleth in me, and I in him. 57 As the living Father hath sent me, and I live by the Father: so he that eateth me, even he shall live by me.
John 6:53-57 (KJV)

Supplies for Survival

If you still have and are able to make purchases, prepare for the darkness that will cover the earth and cause the world to come to a complete standstill. You need to work quickly to gather supplies for survival. Since there will be an increase in wars and violence, you may want to equip your dwellings with some type of weapon in the event you need to protect yourself. You will need to store your food for pack up and go, which is easily accessible in preparation for the unstable weather patterns. Avoid publicizing your storehouse on social media, as you will become a target for theft from people who are desperate and did not properly prepare. As you are carefully planning, here is a list of items to consider until you are evicted from your homes.

☐ One-gallon liquid chlorine bleach.

☐ Battery-powered radio or TV.

☐ Flashlights

☐ Lantern LED

☐ Extra fresh batteries for radio, TV, lantern, and flashlights.

☐ Packs of emergency drinking water and emergency prepackaged dry meals

☐ Solar Powered Generator

☐ Fire extinguisher (small canister A-B-C type).

☐ Freeze dryer for food storage.

☐ A First Aid Kit with bandages, scissors, a tweezer, and Steri-strips for superficial suturing. Over-the-counter medicine such as Tylenol, Ibuprofen, an Antihistamine, wound, antiseptic, and Medi honey to aid in wound healing.

☐ A handbook for health using natural and herbal remedies. Additional tools you will need are as follows:

☐ Rope (for rescue, tow, tying down property)

☐ Shovel

☐ Hammer and nails

☐ Multi-Tool with pliers

☐ 4 in 1 Emergency Tool (with gas and water shut off)

☐ Utility Work gloves

☐ Eye Goggles

☐Utility Tape; electrical tape

☐N-95 particulate masks and a re-usable respirator face mask

☐Disinfecting spray

☐Paper towels

☐Garbage bags with ties

☐Steel toe boots

☐Clothing for extreme cold weather patterns

Exhortation to the 21st Century Church

The diet of the 21st-century church is probably one of the most challenging things to address. We are literally what we eat because the food you put in your mouth breaks down to amino acids that become the building blocks for the recovery of every cell in your body. If you are not eating foods with plenty of vitamins and nutrients, your body lacks the materials to rebuild damaged cells, increasing the risk of cancer and other disease. With the introduction of genetically modified foods and laboratory-made meat, the question still remains: how will these foods that we have never had before affect the amino acid structures for cellular recovery?

Most often, the message of healthy eating in the 21st Century Church was dismissed way too often with excuses like healthy food is too expensive that was used as an excuse to overindulge in foods that have absolutely no nutritional value for your cellular recovery and health and wholeness. The 21st Century Church has failed to fully embrace the concept of health by making the necessary lifestyle changes of the 80/20 healthy eating rule, with eating nutritious foods at 80% and your favorite treats at 20%. Because the church cannot be disciplined with the 80/20 rule, many people suffer from diseases like obesity, diabetes, hypertension, lack of energy, heart disease, and cancer. Excuses have been used for being too tired to meal prep or cook healthy meals when the consequences of sickness and disease are way more costly in time, energy, and money.

If you are a believer and still reading this book, you still have time to implement healthy lifestyle habits so you don't fall victim to a medical system with high healthcare costs, extended wait times from poor access, and delayed care. Your physical body is the most important component to completing your life assignment on Earth because you cannot do anything on Earth without a physical body. Your health is important because you can have a deep desire and passion to serve God, but with your health, there will be limitations to what you will do for God. There is so much information on health available in books, courses, online seminars, and support groups, but the issue is not whether you have the information or the discipline. A healthy life is a matter of choice, and you still have time to choose health so you are able to fulfill the great commission to go into all the world and preach the gospel before the rapture.

The Frequency of Grounding

If you have not heard about the activity grounding, I want to provide a brief explanation and share the importance of finding a safe area for grounding during the tribulation. Grounding, also referred to as earthing, is an activity where your hands or feet have direct contact with the earth. Science research found that when electrical conductivity from the earth comes in contact with the physical body, this activity affects the physiology of the body and its health benefits. Some diseases that were found to be a benefit of grounding were autoimmune diseases, inflammatory diseases, immune system disorders, wound healing, and also beneficial in disease prevention.

Taking into consideration the frequency of health is 62–78-megahertz, grounding would have relevance in the electrical conductivity from the earth, allowing electrons from the earth to spread over the skin to enter the body for a complex reaction, simply put, a recharge. When you examine the activity of grounding and understand God's creation, scientific research on grounding confirms that we are beings of light and energy existing on a planet that is alive and vibrating a frequency. Based on the scriptures in the Bible, the origin of all creation, even our existence, comes from God, the Divine Creator, who is the essence of light.

5 This is the message which we have heard from Him and declare to you, that God is light and in Him is no darkness at all.
1 John 1:5 (NKJV)

In the beginning God created the heavens and the earth.
Genesis 1:1 (NKJV)

When the scripture says God is *light*, in Strong's Concordance, the Greek translation is *Phos,* which is a prefix of the word photon, which is a tiny particle of electromagnetic waves or electromagnetic energy. God is eternal, supreme, and as powerful as an omnipotent God.

Indeed, these are the mere edges of His ways, And how small a whisper we hear of Him!

But the thunder of His power who can understand?"
Job 26:14 (NKJV)

And I heard, as it were, the voice of a great multitude, as the sound of many waters and as the sound of mighty thunder, saying, "Alleluia! For the Lord God Omnipotent reigns! with being made of.
Revelation 19:6 (NKJV)

8 "I am the Alpha and the Omega, *the* Beginning and *the* End," says the Lord, "who is and who was and who is to come, the Almighty.
Revelation 1:8 (NKJV)

22 *But I saw no temple in it, for the Lord God Almighty and the Lamb are its temple.*
Revelation 21:22 (NKJV)

18 *I will be a Father to you, And you shall be My sons and daughters, Says the LORD Almighty.*
2 Corinthians 6:18 (NKJV)

Who is God? God is not an imagery or a distant, far-off supreme being that is disconnected from His creation. God existed before the beginning of all life and is the creator of everything in existence, and everything has its existence in Him. God is everywhere, and He is omnipresent.

While the presence of the Holy Spirit has been removed from the earth in the tribulation, the existence of God remains in every living thing. Before the rapture, God's existence showed through creation in the array of beauty from the sun that shined to warm the skin or a cool breeze that softly stroked the face while sitting on the beach. God's existence is shown through the roaring waves that form on the ocean shores and through the electrons that move from the earth across the skin of your body when you make physical contact with the earth.

Unfortunately, you will no longer experience the beauty of God's existence through nature, but nature will display the suffering from man's rebellion in the birth pains of disasters. As the tribulation progresses, the earth will produce destructive weather patterns with deadly effects. The birth pains from the earth will cause tornadoes, hail, intense heat, thunderstorms, hurricanes, and cosmic earthquakes. In this time of tribulation, the heavens, too, will manifest the Creator's displeasure as stars fall from their celestial thrones and the moon bleeds red, portending the approach of the Day of the Lord. The skies will no longer herald the grace of divine light but will resonate with the sound of celestial trumpets, signaling the imminent final reckoning, as depicted in the apocalyptic visions of John.

All these are but the beginning of the birth pains.
Matthew 24:8 (ESV)

People will flee to underground bunkers-type communities in an attempt to escape the cosmic rays and extreme heat, but there will be nowhere to escape, as the underground bunkers become coffins for masses of people suffocate to death from carbon dioxide poisoning from failed ventilation systems.

15 And the kings of the earth, the great men, [a]the rich men, the commanders, the mighty men, every slave and every free man hid themselves in the caves and in the rocks of the mountains, 16 and said to the mountains and rocks, "Fall on us and hide us from the face of Him who sits on the throne and from the wrath of the Lamb! 17 For the great day of His wrath has come, and who is able to stand? **Revelation 6:15-17 (NKJV)**

During the first half of the tribulation, ¼ of the population will die from widespread violence, plagues, world hunger, and beastly creatures roaming the earth and devouring mankind. Death will spread across the earth, and no one will be safe. Simple tasks such as walking to the mailbox or driving a car will result in death from violent acts like car hijacking and mass shootings occurring in full view of witnesses. Massive death will sweep the globe, and wars against the nations will result in massive bloodshed and death.

And power was given to them over a fourth of the earth, to kill with sword, with hunger, with death, and by the beasts of the earth. **Revelation 8:6c (NKJV)**

As people harden and their anger increases toward God, tribulation believers will be sought out, offering a reward of food and water. No one can be trusted because the virtue of trust from believers will be rare and far between, replaced with a world of darkness and evil. The only trust that will be observable will be the trust from tribulation believers place in God as they stand in faith to profess Jesus as Lord and Savior and refuse the mark of the beast.

The earth's surface once provided a frequency for health, and life will slowly become inhabitable as the earth's ground is seared from intense heat and meteorite storms. The trees will no longer wave their leaves with radiance, and all vegetation will dry up and die from the scorching heat, fires, and windstorms. The water will no longer be the source of life as all the aquatic life in the ocean, seas, and streams die from toxins, and the water turns to a blood consistency. The frequency of life from the earth will disintegrate before your eyes as the earth begins to break apart from astronomical catastrophic events. A catastrophic earthquake will create breaches in the earth's foundation, separating the very ground that has always connected the states. In the final hour of the tribulation, God's wrath will be evident as the earth begins to implode on itself for ruin with an ultimate plan for the earth's complete destruction for the creation of a new heaven and earth. Those remaining on earth will witness the wrath of God for man's attempt to take the place of God as the creator and use the very DNA of His creation to create a superhuman being. The final wrath will be poured on earth because man has rejected and rebelled against God with the aim of superior knowledge through the advanced technology of artificial intelligence. The innocent blood shed at the hands of evil will finally be avenged by God once and for all. The world will come to an end, and all demons will be thrown into hell with the devil, antichrist, and the false prophet.

10 The devil, who deceived them, was cast into the lake of fire and brimstone where[a] the beast and the false prophet are. And they will be tormented day and night forever and ever.

Revelation 20:10 (NKJV)

Exhortation to the 21st Century Church

As I am writing this book, do you know I was so convicted I had to ask myself?

Kimberly, are you really saved? You are writing a book for health for people left behind, but will you be surprised and be left on earth after the rapture? After the rapture, when all your unsaved friends start making phone calls to people they knew who went to church, will they reach your voicemail because you were raptured, or will you pick up your phone because you were left behind? In writing this book, I had to do an inventory. Kimberly, are you really saved, or will you be one of those church people surprised because you were left behind? So, I did an inventory: I read my bible, not a sign, because the devil knows the Bible. I acknowledge Jesus as my Lord and Savior, not a sign because the devil and their demons know Jesus is the Lord and Savior. I go to church, not a sign because demons sit in church every Sunday. I work in the church, which is not a sign you're saved because we see false preachings and sing from pulpits every Sunday. I asked myself, what if all the things we do are a path to Jesus but not the sign you are saved and really belong to Jesus? I am not suggesting you can lose your salvation, but presenting the question, are you really saved?

With all the issues and excuses we make for not being disciplined, the question is, are you really saved? With all the excuses we continue to make about our misbehavior, the question is, are you really saved? I don't believe your lack of discipline is the issue because you can discipline yourself to do everything else. The same discipline it takes to put a bourbon sour to your lips every night is the same discipline to pick up your Bible and read. If you really belong to God, once you set your will to change something in your life for God, power is made available for you to make those changes. The same power that raised Jesus from the dead is available every day to help you overcome that carnal nature. Are you really saved? This struggle between carnal desires and divine obedience echoes Paul's lament in Romans, where he describes the war between doing what he hates and failing to do what he desires. This internal conflict underscores the necessity of grace, as emphasized by Augustine, who argued that divine help is essential not only for living righteously but for willing it in the first place. Thus, the power to overcome is not merely a matter of human effort but a gift of grace, renewing us day by day.

When you are saved for real, there is a transforming power available to those who belong to God, and if you are not experiencing the transforming power where you are bearing fruit, are you really saved? We have held arguments in the church for years on losing one's salvation, but I challenge the argument with the question. If we need to argue, can one lose their salvation because they practice a carnal lifestyle? Are you really saved? I am not talking about making mistakes and repenting, I am referring to the people who choose to live a compromised life with continual disobedience; are you really saved?

Many people in the church who were raised by parents who were stout believers were taught how to be saved but were never really saved in a heart-to-heart experience with God. They practice the church behaviors and religious etiquette of being saved, but they are not really saved.

Unfortunately, after the rapture, the church will not be empty but filled with church people who thought they were saved because many church people have never experienced the love of God that turned them in the direction of repentance.

I was one of those church people raised in a Christian home. My father was a Pastor, and my mother worked alongside him, teaching Bible studies and Sunday school. I was raised in the church and learned to memorize scriptures as a child. I was baptized in the second grade because this was the lifestyle that was practiced as a believer. But I didn't have my heart-to-heart experience with God until I was in the seventh grade. Over 40 years later, I still remember the day I turned my life over to God. My family was attending a church in Oxnard called Oxnard Baptist Temple. In the youth class, we watched the movie "Left Behind," and an altar call was given at the end of the movie. As I stood by and watched other teens flood the altar that Sunday morning, I didn't feel I needed to go forward because I was raised in a Christian home and attended Sunday School every week with a vague memory of being baptized. But on the way home from church that day, the call to Jesus tugged on my heart to the point I became wrestled while riding home. As soon as we arrived home, I remember going straight to my bedroom, closing the door, and kneeling beside my bed to have a heart-to-heart experience with God, and that was when I was really saved.

I have made many mistakes being saved, but my Christian Walk has remained in the direction of following Christ. I remember one occasion when I was 21 years old; after being out on a Saturday night drinking and feeling guilty about my behavior, I told God I wasn't going to follow Him anymore but just live my life. As I was lying on my back looking at the ceiling, I remember a big hand coming through the ceiling and shaking me, leaving me with a reverential fear, being shaken sober to my commitment to a life of repentance with God. The next day, I was in the Sunday service, ready to serve. As an adult, I wanted to be baptized again since my first baptism had come as a result of a Christian family lifestyle that I deeply appreciate. Several years ago, I had a deep desire to follow the ordinance of baptism and asked my husband, Pastor Lonnie, to baptize me in our community pool. That day, my baptism wasn't before crowds of people, but it was before God in a heartfelt desire for obedience. Maybe the problem with the 21st Century church is we have a lot of church people who know the etiquette of religious behavior, but there are very few people in the church who are really saved and have had a specific encounter with the love of God that caused a repented heart for a surrendered life. With the current state of the 21st-century church, after the rapture, the church will still be full of church people who think they are saved.

So, what is the sign that you are really saved? The true sign that you are really saved is repentance, which is more than just acknowledging Jesus and asking for forgiveness. Repentance means to turn away from the sinful lifestyle and turn to God. If you are practicing a sinful lifestyle, are you really saved, or do you wear a label of saved and will be surprised when you are left behind? If you are really saved, you will not brag, boast, and post pictures about you getting lit and turning up, but you will be convicted. If you are really saved, you will be convicted of sin and not make excuses to live in sin. In referencing 1 John 1:6, If we claim to be saved and in fellowship with God but continue to live in sin and darkness, we are probably not saved. If you are really saved, you would not practice disobedience to instructions from God's Word. If you choose to permanently live in disobedience to God's word, you may not really be saved. When you are saved and love God, you will obey His Word. If you are really saved, you would have a desire to be with God and have fellowship with His people more than you desire to party with the world. You would desire to know God more through the disciplines of reading and understanding God's Word. Are you really saved if you could go days without talking to God or only have an experience with God on Sundays? Are you really saved if you could waste precious time gaming and surfing through social media instead of talking to God? Saved people want to spend time with God and fellowship with His people. If you are really saved, you will reject the world's system and carnality instead of indulging in the pleasures of whatever happens in Vegas stays in Vegas. The truth is that whatever happens in Vegas does not stay in Vegas; it is attached to your soul and carried home with you. The truth is while you are dancing and raising your hands at a concert with your favorite music artists with the horns, hand symbols, and stage props designed to resemble a portal, demons are being released to attach to your soul. While you are lifting your hands and dancing before their gods, you are participating in their worship of their god. People who are really saved reject the carnality of the world system and sell out to Christ. People who are really saved don't practice lifestyles with one foot in the world and one foot in the church. If you are really saved, you will not love the world and the things of the world. If you are really saved, you will draw a clear line, having a committed lifestyle as a believer bearing good fruit.

People who are really saved have had a specific encounter with God and can remember that time and hour they experienced God's love and made the decision to turn from their sinful lifestyle to live for God. It's encountering the love of God that brings people to the place of repentance to be saved. It's not learned church behavior, working in ministry, a Christian upbringing, or practicing family religious beliefs and traditions. To be saved, you must have a heart-to-heart encounter with the love of God with repentance that causes you to turn from your sinful ways, surrendering your life to God. Repentance and being saved stem from your love encounter with God, and you demonstrate your love back through a committed lifestyle. If you are not living a committed lifestyle, are you really saved?

If you are reading this and part of the 21st Century Church, you may not be saved. If you were raised in a religious family and taught religious beliefs and behaviors, but you cannot remember a specific time when you had a heart-to-heart experience with the love of God overwhelmed you, causing you to decide to live a surrendered life, you may not be saved. As articulated by leaders like John Wesley, the founder of Methodism, such moments of heartfelt conversion are essential for genuine faith. These transformative experiences are described as the 'new birth,' a spiritual awakening vital for true salvation, reflecting the profound change that must occur within one's heart and soul.

The salvation experience is more than just repeating a prayer so you make it into heaven.

Real salvation only happens when you have an experience with the love of God that permeates every life experience from birth to this very day. Real salvation for a complete about-face into a surrendered lifestyle that pleases God only happens when you understand it was God's love that kept you alive when you cried out for help during the abuse. Salvation comes when you allow God's love to permeate your heart. God was there when you were rejected and left alone to take care of yourself. It was God's love that protected you when you were stealing for drug money to self-medicate your emotional pain. God's love is not an intellectual process of reasoning, but it is a heartfelt experience that brings deep understanding that God was there during the lowest moments of your life. Through all life's disappointments and difficulties, God was there, and He is still here up to this very moment.

Unfortunately, when God gave mankind free will to make their own choices, people make choices that inflict physical harm and emotional pain on their children, family, and others who happen to cross their path. When you were suffering at the hand of your attacker and cried out for help, God couldn't override the will of your attacker, force them to make the right decision, or even make them stop, but God intervened, and He kept you through it all. When you come to the moment when you see it was God's love for you that kept you through it all, His love will overpower you with a heart of gratitude for a surrendered life to God. And it is at this moment you ready to pray the sinner's prayer that goes something like this.

Dear God, thank you for being there and loving me when I didn't know you were there. Forgive me for the sin of rejecting You. Thank you, God, for showing the greatest act of love by sending your Son Jesus to give His life so I can have life eternally in heaven when I die. As I accept the free gift of salvation, I make a heartfelt commitment to live my life for God on earth and share the love of God that I experienced with other people. I receive the gift of salvation and thank you, God, for saving my soul.

The Frequency of Hell and Heaven

Before I even attempt to discuss the frequency of heaven that will encourage you to stand in the face of persecution as they put you to death, let's explore the frequency of hell people will experience if they receive the mark of the beast. During the tribulation, the mark is more than a digitalized number embedded in the hand or forehead for personal identification to buy or sell.

The mark of the beast is a symbol and representation of a mark on the soul of an individual as surrendering your allegiance to Satan, the anti-Christ, and the false prophet. During the tribulation, the system of the anti-Christ will force people to choose either God or Satan with an identification mark on the hand or forehead, and if you refuse the mark, you will be tortured until you surrender or die. If you surrender to the mark of the beast, you will experience the wrath of God throughout eternity.

2 So the first went and poured out his bowl upon the earth, and a foul and loathsome sore came upon the men who had the mark of the beast and those who worshiped his image.
Revelation 16:2 (NKJV)

The wrath of God will be poured out on those who have identified themselves with having the mark of the beast. They will be afflicted with the worst skin lesions ever witnessed in the history of medicine. During the first part of the tribulation, one-fourth of the population will die, and midway through the tribulation, another one-third of the population will die. During the tribulation, you will die from a plague, starvation, a casualty of extreme weather patterns such as an earthquake or flooding, or you will be murdered. If you have the mark of the beast when you die, you will close your eyes to earth only to open your eyes in an even worse condition than what you could ever imagine. If you accept the mark of the beast, you will wake up in a place called hell. Just as Pharaoh's heart was hardened, leading to catastrophic plagues, so too will the end times witness unparalleled tribulations as a sign of God's unyielding justice against iniquity and idolatry. These events serve as a solemn reminder of the relentless pursuit of divine justice and the ultimate destiny awaiting those who defy the Creator's commandments.

8 But the cowardly, unbelieving, abominable, murderers, sexually immoral, sorcerers, idolaters, and all liars shall have their part in the lake which burns with fire and brimstone, which is the second death.
Revelations 21:8 (NKJV)

If everything has a frequency and health is at the frequency of 62–72 megahertz, sickness in the body is suggested to start at 58 megahertz, and death occurs at 28 megahertz. If hell had a frequency, I expect the frequency of hell to be below – 0 or lower. In an environment with a frequency below - 0 megahertz, you will not be able to take a deep breath and will suffer from air hunger. The conditions of an environment at a frequency – 0 or lower would place you in a state of continuous suffocation, but you will never die because you will live in an eternal state of death. Hell will be literally absent of oxygen, and you will never take a breath of fresh air again, but every breath will be sucked from your being.

Not only will the atmosphere vacuum the breath from your lungs, but the smell of hell will be intolerable. I imagine the smell of hell wreaking with the most unpleasant stench known to mankind, with the stink of rotting flesh with a metallic smell of blood mixed with feces and bacteria. The fire and brimstone will cause the atmosphere to be filled with sulfur that will cause intense burning to the eyes, nose, and throat, producing an uncontrollable cough with endless wrenching. The concentrated toxic levels of sulfur in the atmosphere will cause a tightness in your chest that will restrict chest movements to breathe, intensifying the feeling of suffocation.

At a frequency below zero, there will be no light, which means hell will be absolute darkness. The darkness of hell will be so black the density of the atmosphere will have a thickness and weight that crushes against your very being. All light will be blocked by the darkness, and the flames of fire that will never give light or be put out will burn with intense heat, inflicting unfathomable torment. Hell is not a place where you will party with your ride-to-die friends, but it's a place of absolute isolation in darkness with deep chilling sounds that have never been transmitted to mankind's ear in an earth's frequency. In hell, with a frequency below zero, low-pitch-dark sounds never heard before will reverberate soundwaves through the body, causing extreme chills and terror. Fear and terror will dominate the atmosphere of hell, absent of rest periods for recovery. If you take the mark of the beast, your soul will be marked for this place for an eternal state of torment in hell.

*28 And do not fear those who kill the body but cannot kill
the soul. But rather fear Him who is able to destroy both
soul and body in hell.*
Matthew 10:28 (NKJV)

But, if you reject the mark of the beast, they will hate
you. They will find you and torture you in unimaginable
ways because they hate God. In the time and hour when they
find you, do not be afraid but understand to live with Christ
throughout eternity, you must die. When they torture you to
surrender to the mark and acknowledge Satan as Lord, you
must not surrender and take the mark. If you do surrender,
they will still kill you because they are evil. You will need
to stand in your faith and fight the good fight of faith until
the end. God is with you and will help you endure the
suffering and accept you into eternal glory when you die.
The pain and agony of living in this dark, corrupt world will
soon come to an end because it's your time to enter into
eternal glory with God

*10 Therefore I endure all things for the sake of the [c]elect,
that they also may obtain the salvation which is in Christ
Jesus with eternal glory.*
2 Timothy 2:10 (NKJV)

. 21 For to me, to live is Christ, and to die is gain.
Philippians 1:21 (NKJV)

*7 I have fought the good fight, I have finished the race, I
have kept the faith. 8 Finally, there is laid up for me the
crown of righteousness, which the Lord, the righteous
Judge, will give to me on that Day, and not only to me but
also to all who have loved His appearing.*
2 Timothy 4:7-8 (NKJV)

The Frequency of Heaven

I have not had visions of heaven like the Apostle John, who described the chronology of the tribulation and the final judgment with new earth in the Book of Revelation during his prophetic time travel into heaven. I have not had a near-death experience like other people who have shared stories about seeing or experiencing an intense sensation of being pulled into a vortex of completely overwhelming love and acceptance. I have heard some near-death experiences explained as seeing a bright light filled with an overwhelming sense of love. But I will attempt to capture the vibration of heaven through the revelation of the Holy Spirit Apostle John's visions recorded in Revelation chapters 19 through 22. Heaven is a real place with a frequency no one has ever experienced before.

When you die and close your eyes in a permanent sleep on earth, the moment your eyes close in death, in the next blink, you will wake up in eternal glory of the frequency of heaven. It will be a frequency that has never been experienced on Earth or known to man. This frequency is preserved for those people who fought the fight of faith and put their trust in Jesus as their Lord and Savior and did not surrender to the mark. The frequency of heaven is the purest of pure frequency, enveloped in God's limitless love and acceptance. This celestial frequency of heaven aligns with the biblical descriptions found in the Book of Revelation, where John speaks of a new heaven where God will wipe away every tear, and death shall be no more. This vision echoes the divine promise of restoration and perfection, a theme reiterated by prophets like Isaiah, who foretold a future where suffering and pain are replaced by everlasting joy and peace, underpinning the eternal reward for the faithful. Just like hell will have ongoing fear and torment fill the environment, the environment of heaven will be filled with limitless power from God's love and acceptance. Heaven will carry a frequency in the atmosphere that is void of any darkness or negativity.

As you experience the radiant frequencies of heaven, you will be ushered to a place in heaven called the judgment seat. Every day of your life on earth was purposed for this very moment to stand before God and explain what you did for Him with the time while you lived on earth.

10 For we must all appear before the judgment seat of Christ, that each one may receive the things done in the body, according to what he has done, whether good or bad.
2 Corinthians 5:10 (NKJV)

As you stand before God, you will be overtaken by His love and full acceptance. A deep regret will fill your heart as your mind begins to replay every moment and missed opportunity you had to decide to live for God. As you continue to experience deeper levels of God's love pierce every part of your being, you will fall to your knees in ultimate reverence before God. As you kneel before God, perfect illumination will blanket your mind to understand your life purpose in every missed opportunity and missed mark of disobedience. Your mind will be illuminated to see the hand of God orchestrating every offense, trial, conflict, and hurt you experienced on earth for your benefit to share the of Jesus Christ. As you kneel before God in tears, you will be overtaken by deep sorrow, and you will fail to commit fully and trust God. The sorrow will cause a brokenness of heart before God with repentance, deep appreciation, and gratitude, wishing you would have done more for God while living on earth. After you are purged before Going to the judgment seat, every sorrow and hurt you have ever experienced on earth will be wiped clean

4 And God will wipe away every tear from their eyes; there shall be no more death, nor sorrow, nor crying. There shall be no more pain, for the former things have passed away."
Revelation 21:4 (NKJV)

As you kneel surrounded by the love and acceptance of God, He will reward you according to the works you did on earth. You will receive a crown of life for enduring the tribulation and being accepted into eternal glory with Jesus. The crown of life will be presented to you as a reward for your loyal service on earth, persevering through the pressure, and standing in faith in God.

12 Blessed is the man that endured temptation: for when he is tried, he shall receive the crown of life, which the Lord hath promised to them that love him.
James 1:12 (NKJV)

13 Every man's work shall be made manifest: for the day shall declare it, because it shall be revealed by fire; and the fire shall try every man's work of what sort it is.
1 Corinthians 3:13 (NKJV)

Now, let's explore the environment of heaven because heaven must be a magnificent sight with beauty and order.

After you have been purged in the presence of God, you will enter a frequency of heaven with splendor and magnificence. According to Revelation chapter 19, Apostle John witnessed the splendor of the organization of heaven when he saw 24 elders with four living creatures sitting on the throne worshipping God. In this verse, the elders are not referring to an age but a rank of authority over the government of the throne of God in the country of heaven.

4 And the twenty-four elders and the four living creatures fell down and worshiped God who sat on the throne, saying, "Amen! Alleluia!" 5 Then a voice came from the throne, saying, "Praise our God, all you His servants and those who fear Him, both small and great!"
Revelation 19:4,5 (NKJV)

The throne of God in heaven will represent the supreme power and authority of God that reigned before time and will reign forever through eternity. And you will meet the King of kings and the Lord of lords with eyes that burn as a flame of fire clothed in fine white linen. A piece of His clothing dipped in blood will read "The Word of God,' and He will be surrounded by armies of angels on white horses dressed in white linen. On earth, the beast, the kings of the earth, and their armies will make war with the King, but the beast and false prophet that performed miracles and deceived people into taking the mark of the beast and worshipping the image of Satan will be struck down and casts into the lake of fire. The copycat imitation of the trinity with Satan, the false prophet, and the anti-Christ will be thrown into hell. Those that remain on earth will be caught up to stand before God with the Book of Life, and whoever's name is not written in the book will be cast into the lake of fire.

All of nature's birth pain will come to an end as God will create a new heaven and a new earth. The Holy City will descend from the heavens to form the New Jerusalem, where God will dwell and live amongst His people. The Holy City will shine from the glory of God, which will illuminate the skies with the most magnificent colors, such as jasper and crystal. The Holy City will brighten the skies with no need to have a sun or a moon. The walls of the building in the Holy City will be made of pure, transparent gold. The foundation of the buildings will be made of the most precious stones, such as jasper, sapphire, chalcedony, and emerald. A great wall will surround the Holy City, with 12 gates made from one pearl and an angel written on the names of the 12 foundations of the children of Israel. The gates will forever remain open because God's glory rests in the city; there will be no night there. The streets of the Holy City will reflect the shine made from transparent gold.

Those believers who were faithful in service to God while on earth will form the nations that will walk in the light of God, while other believers who served God through the agape sacrificial service will be rewarded as lord of the land as kings of the earth to bring glory to and honor into the Holy City before God. In the Holy City, a pure river of water for life will flow from the holy throne. In the Holy City will be the tree of life that produces 12 fruits every month; the leaves of the tree will represent the permanent healing of the nation, and there will be no curses, sickness, or death. All the servants will serve Him and see His face with His name engraved on our foreheads. And the servants of the Lord shall reign forever and ever with God.

Exhortation to the 21st Century Church

There will be a time when you will have to stand before God to give an account of what you did with your time on earth. As your mind is enlightened to the absolute love and acceptance of God that was with you in every circumstance and the missed opportunity to obey God, a deep reverence and gratitude will flood your heart with regrets of wishing you would have done more for God. You will regret the times you opted to emotionally pull out because you were hurt and offended. You will regret the times you served in ministry but grumbled and complained because things didn't happen the way you wanted. You will regret the wasted time spent in bars and clubs and hours of wasted time spent scrolling on social media. You will regret the compromised lifestyle and not fully committing to personal growth and the great commission to share the love of Jesus with others. You will regret the excuses you made for not taking the gift God gave you to share with the earth and expanding that gift to share Jesus.

Every believer who stands before God will experience this deep regret because the best man could offer will be as a filthy rag before the presence of God. As you stand before God, you will see the times you operated in ego to build your name instead of preaching the name of Jesus. Believers from the 21st Century Church will see that their ministry works were offered in fear and pride rather than as a ministry service to God: their church services were full of religious protocol with the presence of God to move freely absent. The church will finally see the error in seeking an organizational church strategy to grow its church in the absence of intercessory prayer.

But God's love towards us will be never-ending and relentless. God will still love you and accept you into eternal glory, not on your merits of work, but the work of His Son Jesus, who shed His blood and resurrected you into eternal glory with God. Nothing will change God's love and acceptance for you, but the work you do on earth is the merit that will determine how and where you will live throughout eternity in heaven. The work you do or do not do on earth never changes God's love for you, but it determines your inheritance and the Lord's reward.

12 "And behold, I am coming quickly, and My reward is with Me, to give to everyone according to his work.
Revelation 22:12 (NKJV)

Heaven is a magnificent environment of beauty and order, and when God creates the new earth for us to live out eternity, the new earth will be a magnificent environment with beauty and order and eternal assignments based on the works on earth. Unfortunately, we have been so conditioned to accept our current state of life on earth, never realizing real life starts with eternity and the eternal assignment for the new earth will be based on how you walked in your assignment on the previous earth. The concept of divine compensation for earthly deeds resonates across religious and philosophical traditions, underscoring the significance of our actions in shaping our eternal destiny. Such beliefs inspire a steadfast commitment to virtuous living and spiritual growth, anticipating the grandeur of heavenly recompense beyond mortal bounds. Although there are rewards that will be given to you in this life for your service to God with an attitude of love, the eternal rewards are much greater.

*23 And whatever you do, do it heartily, as to the Lord
and not to men, 24 knowing that from the Lord you will
receive the reward of the inheritance; for[a] you serve the
Lord Christ. 25 But he who does wrong will be repaid for
what he has done, and there is no partiality.*
Colossians 3:23-25 (NKJV)

The Frequency of Choice

God is the author and creator of everything, and when God created mankind, His intent was to have a people to love because God is love, and the people would love him back by their own choice and free will. God made Adam and Eve and placed them in a perfect environment in the Garden of Eden. God loved them and gave them every provision and fellowshipped with them daily. But God gave Adam and Eve an opportunity to love Him back by placing a tree in the Garden and instructing them not to eat of that tree.

2 By this, we know that we love the children of God when we love God and keep His commandments.
I John 5: 2, 3 (NKJV)

All the arguments that have been made about the act in the garden were simply related to disobedience. God gave Adam and Eve instructions not to eat one specific food, and Adam and Eve had free choice and free will to love God back through obedience. Although Eve was tricked by the cunning serpent because she experienced the love of God firsthand, she had the opportunity to love God back through her decision to say no to the invitation to the disobedience of sin. Since Adam experienced the love of God daily when he walked and talked with God, Adam had an opportunity to love God back by refusing the enticement of his wife to join him in the sin of disobedience. Adam and Eve's greatest sin ever was the sin of disobedience because they chose not to love God back in spite of the love God showed to them.

36 "Teacher, which is the great commandment in the law?" 37 Jesus said to him, "'You shall love the LORD your

*God with all your heart, with all your soul, and with all
your mind.' 38 This is the first and great commandment.*
Matthew 22:36-38 (NKJV)

When Adam and Eve failed to love God back through
obedience, their sin of disobedience separated them from
the love of God, and it was the seed that germinated and
grew, spreading through all generations for all corruption.
In Christian theology, the narrative of Adam and Eve's
disobedience in the Garden of Eden holds profound
significance, symbolizing humanity's fall from grace and
the subsequent need for redemption. This foundational story
underscores the importance of obedience to God's
commands and the consequences of straying from His will.
However, the teachings of Jesus in the New Testament offer
a pathway to reconciliation, emphasizing the primacy of
love for God as the cornerstone of faithful living. While the
sin of disobedience separated mankind from God, the
humble act of obedience reconciled mankind back to God
through the finished work of Jesus from the whipping to the
cross.

*8 And being found in appearance as a man, He humbled
Himself and became obedient to the point of death, even
the death of the cross.*
Philippians 2:8 (NKJV)

It was the humble act of Jesus to leave the atmosphere of
heaven and come to earth through virgin birth to succumb
to the horrible acts of the crucifixion. Jesus obeyed unto his
death so you can be reconciled back to God and have the
opportunity to have a relationship with God and love Him
back through obedience. Your relationship with God is a

free will choice, loving God back through obedience to instructions in His Word.

15 "If you love Me, you will obey Me.
John 14:15 (NKJV)

You must make a choice, and what you choose should determine how you will live the remaining days on earth and, more importantly, how you will spend eternity. Because you were left behind from the first rapture, the choice you make for God will cost you your life. Because you missed the opportunity to choose the free gift of salvation, you must suffer the consequences of the tribulation and will die of starvation, a violent act, a catastrophic weather event, or you will be tortured to death. But you must still choose if you will stand in faith for God or if you make allegiance to Satan in the anti-Christ system for your livelihood on earth. During the tribulation, you must choose to die to your life on earth for eternal life in heaven or live with life on earth for eternal judgment in hell.

24 "No one can serve two masters; for either he will hate the one and love the other, or else he will be loyal to the one and despise the other. You cannot serve God and mammon.
Matthew 6:24 (NKJV)

The decision will be difficult because demonic forces will come against you to intimidate and scare you. They will strategize against you with intense pressure to accept the mark of the beast. But you must resist and choose God. Unfortunately, your choice to stand in faith for God will release a frequency that will release a scent that attracts demons and beastly creatures. You will not be able to hide, and they will find you and put you to death. But because you made the decision to choose God, your choice will release a frequency that will mark your eternal destination for heaven when you die. During this time, you will literally live or die based on the choices you make, and you must choose wisely. Because you were left behind, your choice for God will require a denying of self and a sacrifice of life, and there is no way around it.

23 Then Jesus said to them all, "If anyone wants to follow Me, he must give up himself and his own desires. He must take up his cross every day and follow Me.
Luke 9:23 (NLV)

Remember, when you choose God, there is an eternal reward from heaven waiting for you. Even though the journey through the tribulation will be the worst fight you will ever face, the eternal reward from choosing God will be worth it all when you are transitioned to heaven and feel the embracing of God's love and acceptance.

Exhortation to the 21st Century Church

If the rapture hasn't taken place, you still have time to make a choice. You still have time to choose to serve God with all your heart, mind, and soul and forsake the temporary worldly pleasures. You still have a choice to focus on eternal rewards and serve God as a king throughout eternity. You still have time to decide to live the rest of your life for God with no compromise, indulging in the temporary pleasures that have eternal consequences.

You need to make a decision that goes beyond accepting Jesus as your Lord and Savior and not being left behind.

You need to decide how you will live throughout eternity. And how you live in eternity has everything to do with your commitment in lifestyle to God while you are on earth. Although hanging out in clubs, cursing, drinking, and other sinful behavior will not keep you from heaven because your works didn't get you to heaven, so your works can't keep you from going to heaven if you are born again. You can be confident that your eternal destination of heaven was secured by the blood of Jesus. So, your sin will not keep you from heaven, but your disobedient, undisciplined lifestyle will keep you from experiencing the rewards of heaven because each person will be rewarded for their works.

When you arrive in heaven, you will stand before the judgment seat of God and explain what you did with your time and the gifts God bestowed upon you. Will you stand with tears of regret before God because you made the decision for worldly pleasures on most weekends rather than prepare your heart to be a true worshipper of God in church? Will you stand before God with inexcusable excuses why you write the song, serve on a ministry team, feed the homeless, or simply show up to church? Will you cry in remorse because you missed the opportunity to minister to people because you viewed them for personal use and not a Godly purpose?

We can never lose focus on the fact that when God allows people to come across the path of a believer, the primary purpose of the connection is for teaching, discipleship, fellowship, and worship. The 21st Century Church has failed to fulfill the intended purpose of the church because they have settled on just going to church. We have massaged the egos of the compromised lifestyles, creating a grey area of lukewarmness because we didn't know how to love them without judging them. We never sought the wisdom of God in prayer on how to correct the behavior without breaking the spirit, so we allowed them in positions of leadership that compromised the witness and integrity of the church.

But we still have time to get it right. We still have time to be the church that church that is an adorned bride without spot or blemish when Jesus comes. But we must choose individually and collectively. We must draw a line and choose to commit to live for God. We must be a church that turns from the sin of judgment, criticism, and compromise to seek the Lord's direction and be a church that will be glorified in the last hour. We must be a church that rises up to take place in authority to fulfill the great commission to bring as many people as possible to Jesus before the rapture. The church must experience a revival.

This moves for the revival of the 21st-century Church must start first on an individual level with personal commitment as a believer with a committed lifestyle that exemplifies the message of Jesus. As personal commitments are made, we must move to a collective commitment as a church and then a global revival at the Body of Christ. Jesus is coming back soon, and it is time for a revival of the 21st Century Church. It can start today when it starts with you.

Prayer for Salvation

If you have never said the sinner's prayer and you are not sure about your eternal destination, please understand that God loves you and has been waiting for you. God saw your life before you were born and knew every mishap and mistake before you made it, and He still loves you. There is nothing you can do to prevent God from loving you. And because God loves you, He wants you to decide to spend eternity with Him in eternal paradise when you die. It is your choice. If you choose God, please pray the sinner's prayer below.

Dear God in Heaven. Thank you for loving me and giving me the best heaven could offer by sending your only begotten Son, Jesus. I am a sinner and in need of a Savior. I want to live the rest of my life on earth for God and live in heaven in eternity. Please forgive me for my sins. I believe Jesus died on the cross and was resurrected from the grave so I may have a relationship with God. I ask Jesus to come into my life and come into my heart and save me from my life of destruction. I receive Jesus, and when I die, I believe I will open my eyes to the eternal destiny of heaven. I ask Jesus to help me live a life that is pleasing before God and a testimony to share the message of the gospel with others. In Jesus Name, Amen.